LINCOLN
A PHOTOBIOGRAPHY

Lincoln and his son Tad, 1864.

RUSSELL FREEDMAN

LINCOLN
A PHOTOBIOGRAPHY

ILLUSTRATED WITH PHOTOGRAPHS AND PRINTS

Clarion Books
New York

Sources of photographs and prints are cited on page 144.

Clarion Books
a Houghton Mifflin Company imprint
215 Park Avenue South, New York, NY 10003
Copyright © 1987 by Russell Freedman

For information about permission to reproduce
selections from this book write to Permissions,
Houghton Mifflin Company, 215 Park Avenue South, New York, NY 10003.

Book design by Sylvia Frezzolini
Printed in the U.S.A.

Library of Congress Cataloging-in-Publication Data
Freedman, Russell.   Lincoln.
Bibliography: p.   Includes index.   Summary: Photographs and text trace the life of the Civil War President.
1. Lincoln, Abraham, 1809–1865—Juvenile literature. 2. Presidents—United States—Biography—Juvenile
literature. [1. Lincoln, Abraham, 1809–1865. 2. Presidents] I. Title.
E457.905.F73   1987   973.7′092′4 [B] [92]   86–33379
ISBN 0-89919-380-3   PA ISBN 0-395-51848-2

HC HOR PAP CRW 20 19 18 17 16 15 14 13

For Evans

Contents

As I would not be a slave, so I
would not be a master. This ex=
presses my idea of democracy. —
Whatever differs from this, to the
extent of the difference, is no
democracy. —

A. Lincoln—

The presidential candidate, June 1860. Of this photograph Lincoln said, "That looks better and expresses me better than any I have ever seen; if it pleases the people, I am satisfied."

ONE

The Mysterious Mr. Lincoln

"If any personal description of me is thought desirable, it may be said, I am, in height, six feet, four inches, nearly; lean in flesh, weighing, on average, one hundred and eighty pounds; dark complexion, with coarse black hair and grey eyes—no other marks or brands recollected."

Abraham Lincoln wasn't the sort of man who could lose himself in a crowd. After all, he stood six feet four inches tall, and to top it off, he wore a high silk hat.

His height was mostly in his long bony legs. When he sat in a chair, he seemed no taller than anyone else. It was only when he stood up that he towered above other men.

At first glance, most people thought he was homely. Lincoln thought so too, referring once to his "poor, lean, lank face." As a young man he was sensitive about his gawky looks, but in time, he learned to laugh at himself. When a rival called him "two-faced" during a political debate, Lincoln replied: "I leave it to my audience. If I had another face, do you think I'd wear this one?"

According to those who knew him, Lincoln was a man of many

faces. In repose, he often seemed sad and gloomy. But when he began to speak, his expression changed. "The dull, listless features dropped like a mask," said a Chicago newspaperman. "The eyes began to sparkle, the mouth to smile, the whole countenance was wreathed in animation, so that a stranger would have said, 'Why, this man, so angular and solemn a moment ago, is really handsome!'"

Lincoln was the most photographed man of his time, but his friends insisted that no photo ever did him justice. It's no wonder. Back then, cameras required long exposures. The person being photographed had to "freeze" as the seconds ticked by. If he blinked an eye, the picture would be blurred. That's why Lincoln looks so stiff and formal in his photos. We never see him laughing or joking.

Artists and writers tried to capture the "real" Lincoln that the camera missed, but something about the man always escaped them. His changeable features, his tones, gestures, and expressions, seemed to defy description.

Today it's hard to imagine Lincoln as he really was. And he never cared to reveal much about himself. In company he was witty and talkative, but he rarely betrayed his inner feelings. According to William Herndon, his law partner, he was "the most secretive—reticent—shut-mouthed man that ever lived."

In his own time, Lincoln was never fully understood even by his closest friends. Since then, his life story has been told and retold so many times, he has become as much a legend as a flesh-and-blood human being. While the legend is based on truth, it is only partly true. And it hides the man behind it like a disguise.

The legendary Lincoln is known as Honest Abe, a humble man of the people who rose from a log cabin to the White House. There's no doubt that Lincoln was a poor boy who made good.

Wearing his familiar stovepipe hat, Lincoln towers above General George B. McClellan and his staff during a visit to Fifth Corps headquarters near Sharpsburg, Maryland, October 3, 1862.

And it's true that he carried his folksy manners and homespun speech to the White House with him. He said "howdy" to visitors and invited them to "stay a spell." He greeted diplomats while wearing carpet slippers, called his wife "mother" at receptions, and told bawdy jokes at cabinet meetings.

Lincoln may have seemed like a common man, but he wasn't. His friends agreed that he was one of the most ambitious people they had ever known. Lincoln struggled hard to rise above his log-cabin origins, and he was proud of his achievements. By the time he ran for president he was a wealthy man, earning a large income from his law practice and his many investments. As for the nickname Abe, he hated it. No one who knew him well ever called him Abe to his face. They addressed him as Lincoln or Mr. Lincoln.

Lincoln is often described as a sloppy dresser, careless about his appearance. In fact, he patronized the best tailor in Springfield, Illinois, buying two suits a year. That was at a time when many men lived, died, and were buried in the same suit.

It's true that Lincoln had little formal "eddication," as he would have pronounced it. Almost everything he "larned" he taught himself. All his life he said "thar" for *there*, "git" for *get*, "kin" for *can*. Even so, he became an eloquent public speaker who could hold a vast audience spellbound, and a great writer whose finest phrases still ring in our ears. He was known to sit up late into the night, discussing Shakespeare's plays with White House visitors.

He was certainly a humorous man, famous for his rollicking stories. But he was also moody and melancholy, tormented by long and frequent bouts of depression. Humor was his therapy. He relied on his yarns, a friend observed, to "whistle down sadness."

He had a cool, logical mind, trained in the courtroom, and a practical, commonsense approach to problems. Yet he was deeply superstitious, a believer in dreams, omens, and visions.

We admire Lincoln today as an American folk hero. During the Civil War, however, he was the most unpopular president the nation had ever known. His critics called him a tyrant, a hick, a stupid baboon who was unfit for his office. As commander in chief of the armed forces, he was denounced as a bungling amateur who meddled in military affairs he knew nothing about. But he also had his supporters. They praised him as a farsighted statesman, a military mastermind who engineered the Union victory.

Lincoln is best known as the Great Emancipator, the man who freed the slaves. Yet he did not enter the war with that idea in mind. "My paramount object in this struggle *is* to save the Union," he said in 1862, "and is *not* either to save or destroy slavery." As the war continued, Lincoln's attitude changed. Eventually he came to regard the conflict as a moral crusade to wipe out the sin of slavery.

No black leader was more critical of Lincoln than the fiery abolitionist writer and editor Frederick Douglass. Douglass had grown up as a slave. He had won his freedom by escaping to the North. Early in the war, impatient with Lincoln's cautious leadership, Douglass called him "preeminently the white man's president, entirely devoted to the welfare of white men." Later, Douglass changed his mind and came to admire Lincoln. Several years after the war, he said this about the sixteenth president:

"His greatest mission was to accomplish two things: first, to save his country from dismemberment and ruin; and, second, to free his country from the great crime of slavery. . . . taking him for all in all, measuring the tremendous magnitude of the work before him, considering the necessary means to ends, and surveying the end from the beginning, infinite wisdom has seldom sent any man into the world better fitted for his mission than Abraham Lincoln."

I was born Feb. 12. 1809, in Hardin County, Kentucky.
My parents were both born in Virginia, of undistin=
guished families — second families, perhaps I should say — My mother, who died in my
tenth year, was of a family of the name of Hanks,
some of whom now reside in Adams, and others
in Macon counties, Illinois — My paternal grand=
father, Abraham Lincoln, emigrated from Rock=
ingham County, Virginia, to Kentucky, about 1781 or
2, where, a year or two later, he was killed by
indians, not in battle, but by stealth, when he
was laboring to open a farm in the forest —
His ancestors, who were quakers, went to Virginia
from Berks County, Pennsylvania — An effort to
identify them with the New England family of the same name
ended in nothing more definite, than a similarity
of Christian names in both families, such as
Enoch, Levi, Mordecai, Solomon, Abraham, and
the like —
My father, at the death of his father, was
but six years of age; and he grew up,
litterally without education — He removed
from Kentucky to what is now Spencer county, Indi=
ana, in my eighth year — We reached our new home

Lincoln wrote this autobiographical sketch in 1859.

❧ TWO ❧

A Backwoods Boy

"It is a great piece of folly to attempt to make anything out of my early life. It can all be condensed into a simple sentence, and that sentence you will find in Gray's Elegy*—'the short and simple annals of the poor.' That's my life, and that's all you or anyone else can make out of it."*

Abraham Lincoln never liked to talk much about his early life. A poor backwoods farm boy, he grew up swinging an ax on frontier homesteads in Kentucky, Indiana, and Illinois.

He was born near Hodgenville, Kentucky, on February 12, 1809, in a log cabin with one window, one door, a chimney, and a hard-packed dirt floor. His parents named him after his pioneer grand-father. The first Abraham Lincoln had been shot dead by hostile Indians in 1786, while planting a field of corn in the Kentucky wilderness.

Young Abraham was still a toddler when his family packed their belongings and moved to another log-cabin farm a few miles north, on Knob Creek. That was the first home he could remember, the place where he ran and played as a barefoot boy.

He remembered the bright waters of Knob Creek as it tumbled

From a log cabin to the White House. A replica of Lincoln's Kentucky birthplace.

past the Lincoln cabin and disappeared into the Kentucky hills. Once he fell into the rushing creek and almost drowned before he was pulled out by a neighbor boy. Another time he caught a fish and gave it to a passing soldier.

Lincoln never forgot the names of his first teachers—Zachariah Riney followed by Caleb Hazel—who ran a windowless log schoolhouse two miles away. It was called a "blab school." Pupils of all ages sat on rough wooden benches and bawled out their lessons aloud. Abraham went there with his sister Sarah, who was two years older, when they could be spared from their chores at home. Holding hands, they would walk through scrub trees and across creek bottoms to the schoolhouse door. They learned their numbers from one to ten, and a smattering of reading, writing, and spelling.

Their parents couldn't read or write at all. Abraham's mother, Nancy, signed her name by making a shakily drawn mark. He would remember her as a thin, sad-eyed woman who labored beside her husband in the fields. She liked to gather the children around her in the evening to recite prayers and Bible stories she had memorized.

His father, Thomas, was a burly, barrel-chested farmer and carpenter who had worked hard at homesteading since marrying Nancy Hanks in 1806. A sociable fellow, his greatest pleasure was to crack jokes and swap stories with his chums. With painful effort, Thomas Lincoln could scrawl his name. Like his wife, he had grown up without education, but that wasn't unusual in those days. He supported his family by living off his own land, and he watched for a chance to better himself.

In 1816, Thomas decided to pull up stakes again and move north to Indiana, which was about to join the Union as the nation's nineteenth state. Abraham was seven. He remembered the one hundred-mile journey as the hardest experience of his life. The family set out on a cold morning in December, loading all their possessions on two horses. They crossed the Ohio River on a makeshift ferry, traveled through towering forests, then hacked a path through tangled underbrush until they reached their new homesite near the backwoods community of Little Pigeon Creek.

Thomas put up a temporary winter shelter—a crude, three-sided lean-to of logs and branches. At the open end, he kept a fire burning to take the edge off the cold and scare off the wild animals. At night, wrapped in bearskins and huddled by the fire,

Thomas Lincoln.
This undated photograph is
traditionally accepted as a
portrait of Lincoln's father.

Abraham and Sarah listened to wolves howl and panthers scream.

Abraham passed his eighth birthday in the lean-to. He was big for his age, "a tall spider of a boy," and old enough to handle an ax. He helped his father clear the land. They planted corn and pumpkin seeds between the tree stumps. And they built a new log cabin, the biggest one yet, where Abraham climbed a ladder and slept in a loft beneath the roof.

Soon after the cabin was finished, some of Nancy's kinfolk arrived. Her aunt and uncle with their adopted son Dennis had decided to follow the Lincolns to Indiana. Dennis Hanks became an extra hand for Thomas and a big brother for Abraham, someone to run and wrestle with.

A year later, Nancy's aunt and uncle lay dead, victims of the dreaded "milk sickness" (now known to be caused by a poisonous plant called white snake root). An epidemic of the disease swept through the Indiana woods in the summer of 1818. Nancy had nursed her relatives until the end, and then she too came down with the disease. Abraham watched his mother toss in bed with chills, fever, and pain for seven days before she died at the age of thirty-four. "She knew she was going to die," Dennis Hanks recalled. "She called up the children to her dying side and told them to be good and kind to their father, to one another, and to the world."

Thomas built a coffin from black cherry wood, and nine-year-old Abraham whittled the pegs that held the wooden planks together. They buried Nancy on a windswept hill, next to her aunt and uncle. Sarah, now eleven, took her mother's place, cooking, cleaning, and mending clothes for her father, brother, and cousin Dennis in the forlorn and lonely cabin.

Thomas Lincoln waited for a year. Then he went back to Kentucky to find himself a new wife. He returned in a four-horse wagon with a widow named Sarah Bush Johnston, her three children, and all her household goods. Abraham and his sister were fortunate, for their stepmother was a warm and loving person. She took the motherless children to her heart and raised them as her own. She also spruced up the neglected Lincoln cabin, now shared by eight people who lived, ate, and slept in a single smoky room with a loft.

Abraham was growing fast, shooting up like a sunflower, a spindly youngster with big bony hands, unruly black hair, a dark complexion, and luminous gray eyes. He became an expert with the ax, working alongside his father, who also hired him out to work for others. For twenty-five cents a day, the boy dug wells, built pigpens, split fence rails, felled trees. "My how he could chop!"

Sarah Bush Lincoln. The only surviving photograph of Lincoln's stepmother, taken about 1865 when she was seventy-seven.

exclaimed a friend. "His ax would flash and bite into a sugar tree or a sycamore, and down it would come. If you heard him felling trees in a clearing, you would say there were three men at work, the way the trees fell."

Meanwhile, he went to school "by littles," a few weeks one winter, maybe a month the next. Lincoln said later that all his schooling together "did not amount to one year." Some fragments of his schoolwork still survive, including a verse that he wrote in his homemade arithmetic book: "Abraham Lincoln/his hand and pen/he will be good but/god knows When."

Mostly, he educated himself by borrowing books and newspapers. There are many stories about Lincoln's efforts to find enough books to satisfy him in that backwoods country. Those he

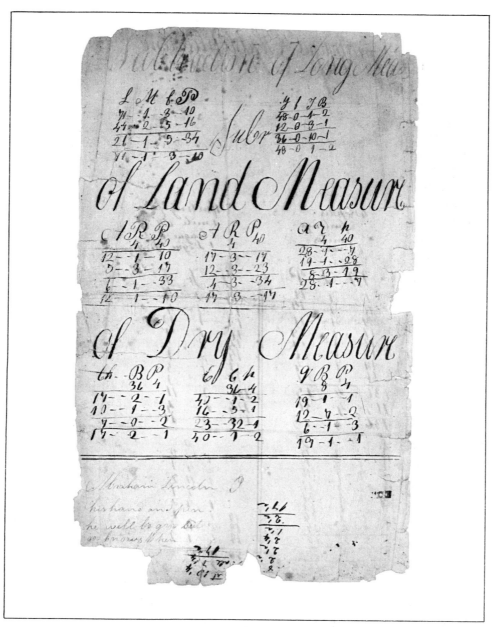

A page from Lincoln's homemade copybook. At the bottom of the page, he wrote four lines of verse in his careful penmanship—the earliest known specimen of his handwriting.

liked he read again and again, losing himself in the adventures of *Robinson Crusoe* or the magical tales of *The Arabian Nights*. He was thrilled by a biography of George Washington, with its stirring account of the Revolutionary War. And he came to love the rhyme and rhythm of poetry, reciting passages from Shakespeare or the Scottish poet Robert Burns at the drop of a hat. He would carry a book out to the field with him, so he could read at the end of each plow furrow, while the horse was getting its breath. When noon came, he would sit under a tree and read while he ate. "I never saw Abe after he was twelve that he didn't have a book in his hand or in his pocket," Dennis Hanks remembered. "It didn't seem natural to see a feller read like that."

By the time he was sixteen, Abraham was six feet tall—"the gangliest awkwardest feller . . . he appeared to be all joints," said a neighbor. He may have looked awkward, but hard physical labor had given him a tough, lean body with muscular arms like steel cables. He could grab a woodsman's ax by the handle and hold it straight out at arm's length. And he was one of the best wrestlers and runners around.

He also had a reputation as a comic and storyteller. Like his father, Abraham was fond of talking and listening to talk. About this time he had found a book called *Lessons in Elocution*, which offered advice on public speaking. He practiced before his friends, standing on a tree stump as he entertained them with fiery imitations of the roving preachers and politicians who often visited Little Pigeon Creek.

Folks liked young Lincoln. They regarded him as a good-humored, easy-going boy—a bookworm maybe, but smart and willing to oblige. Yet even then, people noticed that he could be moody and withdrawn. As a friend put it, he was "witty, sad, and reflective by turns."

At the age of seventeen, Abraham left home for a few months to work as a ferryman's helper on the Ohio River. He was eighteen when his sister Sarah died early in 1828, while giving birth to her first child.

That spring, Abraham had a chance to get away from the backwoods and see something of the world. A local merchant named James Gentry hired Lincoln to accompany his son Allen on a twelve hundred-mile flatboat voyage to New Orleans. With their cargo of country produce, the two boys floated down the Ohio River and into the Mississippi, maneuvering with long poles to avoid snags and sandbars, and to navigate in the busy river traffic.

Lincoln as a flatboatman on the Mississippi River. From an old engraving by H. Brown.

New Orleans was the first real city they had ever seen. Their eyes must have popped as the great harbor came into view, jammed with the masts of sailing ships from distant ports all over the world. The city's cobblestone streets teemed with sailors, traders, and adventurers speaking strange languages. And there were gangs of slaves everywhere. Lincoln would never forget the sight of black men, women, and children being driven along in chains and auctioned off like cattle. In those days, New Orleans had more than two hundred slave dealers.

The boys sold their cargo and their flatboat and returned upriver by steamboat. Abraham earned twenty-four dollars—a good bit of money at the time—for the three-month trip. He handed the money over to his father, according to law and custom.

Thomas Lincoln was thinking about moving on again. Lately he had heard glowing reports about Illinois, where instead of forests there were endless prairies with plenty of rich black soil. Early in 1830, Thomas sold his Indiana farm. The Lincolns piled everything they owned into two ox-drawn wagons and set out over muddy roads, with Abraham, just turned twenty-one, driving one of the wagons himself. They traveled west to their new homesite in central Illinois, not far from Decatur. Once again, Abraham helped his father build a cabin and start a new farm.

He stayed with his family through their first prairie winter, but he was getting restless. He had met an enterprising fellow named Denton Offutt, who wanted him to take another boatload of cargo down the river to New Orleans. Abraham agreed to make the trip with his stepbrother, John Johnston, and a cousin, John Hanks.

When he returned to Illinois three months later, he paid a quick farewell visit to his father and stepmother. Abraham was twenty-two now, of legal age, free to do what he wanted. His parents were settled and could get along without him. Denton Offutt was planning to open a general store in the flourishing village of New Salem, Illinois, and he had promised Lincoln a steady job.

Lincoln arrived in New Salem in July 1831 wearing a faded cotton shirt and blue jeans too short for his long legs—a "friendless, uneducated, penniless boy," as he later described himself. He tended the counter at Denton Offutt's store and slept in a room at the back.

The village stood in a wooded grove on a bluff above the Sangamon River. Founded just two years earlier, it had about one hundred people living in one- and two-room log houses. Cattle grazed behind split-rail fences, hogs snuffled along dusty lanes, and chickens and geese flapped about underfoot. New Salem was still a small place, but it was growing. The settlers expected it to become a frontier boom town.

The reconstructed village of New Salem as it appears today. In the foreground is a split-rail fence.

This New Salem general store was the center of village life.

With his gifts for swapping stories and making friends, Lincoln fit easily into the life of the village. He showed off his skill with an ax, competed in footraces, and got along with everyone from Mentor Graham, the schoolmaster, to Jack Armstrong, the leader of a rowdy gang called the Clary's Grove boys. Armstrong was the wrestling champion of New Salem. He quickly challenged Lincoln to a match.

On the appointed day, an excited crowd gathered down by the river, placing bets as the wrestlers stripped to the waist for combat. They circled each other, then came to grips, twisting and tugging until they crashed to the ground with Lincoln on top. As he pinned Armstrong's shoulders to the ground, the other Clary's Grove boys dived in to join the scuffle. Lincoln broke away, backed against a cliff, and defiantly offered to take them all on—one at a time. Impressed, Armstrong jumped to his feet and offered Lincoln his hand, declaring the match a draw. After that, they were fast friends.

Lincoln also found a place among the town's intellectuals. He joined the New Salem Debating Society, which met once a week in James Rutledge's tavern. The first time he debated, he seemed nervous. But as he began to speak in his high, reedy voice, he surprised everyone with the force and logic of his argument. "He was already a fine speaker," one debater recalled. "All he lacked was culture."

Lincoln was self-conscious about his meagre education, and ambitious to improve himself. Mentor Graham, the schoolmaster

Jack Armstrong,
leader of the "Clary's Grove boys."

Mentor Graham,
the New Salem schoolmaster.

and a fellow debater, took a liking to the young man, lent him books, and offered to coach him in the fine points of English grammar. Lincoln had plenty of time to study. There wasn't much business at Offutt's store, so he could spend long hours reading as he sat behind the counter.

When the store failed in 1832, Offutt moved on to other schemes. Lincoln had to find something else to do. At the age of twenty-three, he decided to run for the Illinois state legislature. Why not? He knew everyone in town, people liked him, and he was rapidly gaining confidence as a public speaker. His friends urged him to run, saying that a bright young man could go far in politics. So Lincoln announced his candidacy and his political platform. He was in favor of local improvements, like better roads and canals. He had made a study of the Sangamon River, and he proposed that it be dredged and cleared so steamboats could call at New Salem—insuring a glorious future for the town.

Before he could start his campaign, an Indian war flared up in northern Illinois. Chief Black Hawk of the Sauk and Fox tribes had crossed the Mississippi, intending, he said, to raise corn on land that had been taken from his people thirty years earlier. The white settlers were alarmed, and the governor called for volunteers to stop the invasion. Lincoln enlisted in a militia company made up of his friends and neighbors. He was surprised and pleased when the men elected him as their captain, with Jack Armstrong as first sergeant. His troops drilled and marched, but they never did sight any hostile Indians. Years later, Lincoln would joke about his three-month stint as a military man, telling how he survived "a good many bloody battles with mosquitoes."

By the time he returned to New Salem, election day was just two weeks off. He jumped into the campaign—pitching horseshoes with voters, speaking at barbecues, chatting with farmers in the fields, joking with customers at country stores. He lost, finishing eighth in a field of thirteen. But in his own precinct, where folks knew him, he received 227 votes out of 300 cast.

Defeated as a politician, he decided to try his luck as a frontier merchant. With a fellow named William Berry as his partner, Lincoln operated a general store that sold everything from axes to beeswax. But the two men showed little aptitude for business, and

Interior of the general store owned by Lincoln and his partner, William Berry.

their store finally "winked out," as Lincoln put it. Then Berry died, leaving Lincoln saddled with a $1,100 debt—a gigantic amount for someone who had never earned more than a few dollars a month. Lincoln called it "the National Debt," but he vowed to repay every cent. He spent the next fifteen years doing so.

To support himself, he worked at all sorts of odd jobs. He split fence rails, hired himself out as a farmhand, helped at the local gristmill. With the help of friends, he was appointed postmaster of New Salem, a part-time job that paid about fifty dollars a year. Then he was offered a chance to become deputy to the local surveyor. He knew nothing about surveying, so he bought a compass, a chain, and a couple of textbooks on the subject. Within six weeks, he had taught himself enough to start work—laying out roads and townsites, and marking off property boundaries.

As he traveled about the county, making surveys and delivering mail to faraway farms, people came to know him as an honest and dependable fellow. Lincoln could be counted on to witness a contract, settle a boundary dispute, or compose a letter for folks who couldn't write much themselves. For the first time, his neighbors began to call him "Abe."

In 1834, Lincoln ran for the state legislature again. This time he placed second in a field of thirteen candidates, and was one of four men elected to the Illinois House of Representatives from Sangamon County. In November, wearing a sixty-dollar tailor-made suit he had bought on credit, the first suit he had ever owned, the twenty-five-year-old legislator climbed into a stagecoach and set out for the state capital in Vandalia.

In those days, Illinois lawmakers were paid three dollars a day to cover their expenses, but only while the legislature was in session. Lincoln still had to earn a living. One of his fellow representatives, a rising young attorney named John Todd Stuart, urged

Lincoln the Rail Splitter. *Painting by J. L. G. Ferris.*

Lincoln to take up the study of law. As Stuart pointed out, it was an ideal profession for anyone with political ambitions.

And in fact, Lincoln had been toying with the idea of becoming a lawyer. For years he had hung around frontier courthouses, watching country lawyers bluster and strut as they cross-examined witnesses and delivered impassioned speeches before juries. He had sat on juries himself, appeared as a witness, drawn up legal documents for his neighbors. He had even argued a few cases before the local justice of the peace.

Yes, the law intrigued him. It would give him a chance to rise in the world, to earn a respected place in the community, to live by his wits instead of by hard physical labor.

Yet Lincoln hesitated, unsure of himself because he had so little formal education. That was no great obstacle, his friend Stuart kept telling him. In the 1830s, few American lawyers had ever seen the inside of a law school. Instead, they "read law" in the office of a practicing attorney until they knew enough to pass their exams.

Lincoln decided to study entirely on his own. He borrowed some law books from Stuart, bought others at an auction, and began to read and memorize legal codes and precedents. Back in New Salem, folks would see him walking down the road, reciting aloud from one of his law books, or lying under a tree as he read, his long legs stretched up the trunk. He studied for nearly three years before passing his exams and being admitted to practice on March 1, 1837.

By then, the state legislature was planning to move from Vandalia to Springfield, which had been named the new capital of Illinois. Lincoln had been elected to a second term in the legislature. And he had accepted a job as junior partner in John Todd Stuart's Springfield law office.

In April, he went back to New Salem for the last time to pack his belongings and say good-bye to his friends. The little village was declining now. Its hopes for growth and prosperity had vanished when the Sangamon River proved too treacherous for steamboat travel. Settlers were moving away, seeking brighter prospects elsewhere.

By 1840, New Salem was a ghost town. It would have been forgotten completely if Abraham Lincoln hadn't gone there to live when he was young, penniless, and ambitious.

Lincoln as a thirty-seven-year-old prairie lawyer in 1846. This daguerreotype is the earliest known camera portrait of Lincoln.

Mary Lincoln as a twenty-eight-year-old wife and mother in 1846. The Lincolns had been married for four years and had two sons when they sat for these companion portraits. "They are very precious to me," Mary said later, "taken when we were young and so desperately in love."

THREE

Law and Politics

"I had studied law, and removed to Springfield to practice it."

Lincoln was twenty-eight years old when he rode into Springfield on a borrowed horse with seven dollars in his pocket. At first he slept on a couch in his partner's law office. Then he met Joshua Speed, a genial young merchant who owned a general store in the center of town.

Speed thought that Lincoln was one of the saddest-looking fellows he had ever laid eyes on. "I never saw so gloomy and melancholy a face in my life," he declared. But he liked the strapping backwoods attorney and invited him to share his room above the store. Lincoln collected his saddlebags, climbed the stairs to Speed's room, tossed the bags on the floor, and said with a grin, "Well Speed, I'm moved!"

Speed's store was a meeting place for a group of bachelors who gathered around a big fireplace several evenings a week to swap stories and argue politics. One of them was a scrappy little attorney named Stephen A. Douglas. From their first meeting, Lincoln and Douglas had plenty to argue about. The leading political parties at the time were the Whigs, who favored a strong government in Washington to guide the nation's future, and the Democrats, who said that the states should control their own affairs, without interference from Washington. Douglas was a Democrat, Lincoln a Whig. They became instant rivals.

Lincoln was ambitious to get ahead. His partner coached him in the fine points of courtroom law, and together they built one of the busiest practices in Springfield. Meanwhile, Lincoln rose rapidly as a Whig party leader. He won reelection to the legislature in 1838 and again in 1840—serving four terms altogether. He was appointed to the party's State Central Committee, which picked candidates for statewide office. And he became an influential member of the Young Whigs, who carried on a running debate with the Young Democrats, led by Stephen Douglas.

He also fell in love—apparently for the first time in his life. Legend tells us that Lincoln once had a tragic love affair with Ann Rutledge, daughter of the New Salem tavern owner, who died at the age of twenty-two. While this story has become part of American folklore, there isn't a shred of evidence that Lincoln ever had a romantic attachment with Ann. Historians believe that they were just good friends.

While Lincoln was still living in New Salem, he carried on a half-hearted courtship with Mary Owens, but that came to nothing. As far as we know, Lincoln never really lost his head over a woman until he met Mary Ann Todd, the pampered and temperamental daughter of a wealthy Kentucky banker.

Lincoln was thirty when they met, Mary almost twenty-one.

Downtown Springfield, where Lincoln practiced law, as it appeared in the 1850s. The street is paved with split logs laid flat side up, and the sidewalk is built of wooden planks.

She had come to Springfield to live with her sister and brother-in-law, Elizabeth and Ninian Edwards, and to find a suitable match among the town's eligible bachelors. The Edwards's elegant hilltop mansion was a popular meeting place for Springfield's political leaders and social elite. Lincoln visited the house with his law partner, a cousin of Elizabeth's.

He met Mary in the winter of 1839. She was witty, vivacious, and stylish, "the very creature of excitement," as a friend described her. She spoke fluent French, recited poetry, knew all the latest dances, was fascinated by politics, and had outspoken views on just about everything. Lincoln was dazzled by the popular Kentucky belle, and Mary was drawn to him.

To many, it seemed an unlikely match. Lincoln knew his way around the brawling political circles of Springfield, but he was still an unpolished fellow from the backwoods, ill at ease in the sophisticated drawing rooms of Springfield high society. Ninian Edwards considered him "a mighty rough man." But Mary saw great promise in Lincoln. She admired his ambition, and beneath his awkward shyness, she found an appealing intensity. He had "the most congenial mind" she had ever met.

As for Lincoln, he had never met anyone like Mary. In her company, he forgot his uncertain manners and felt at ease. He could talk to her as to no one else. By the summer of 1840, they were courting in earnest, Lincoln standing tall and lean beside Mary's short, fashionably plump figure in drawing rooms all over town. By Christmas, they were engaged.

Mary's sister and brother-in-law did not approve. Lincoln was a useful political ally, perhaps, but he was hardly a suitable husband for a member of the eminent Todd family. Elizabeth didn't like him at all. "He never scarcely said a word," she complained, because he "could not hold a lengthy conversation with a lady—

Elizabeth and Ninian Edwards, Lincoln's influential in-laws. They tried to prevent the marriage.

was not sufficiently educated and intelligent in the female line to do so." The Edwardses looked down on Lincoln as a social climber—a gangly country bumpkin who never spoke about his origins. He lived in a room above a store. He was deeply in debt. Mary could do better than that. Lincoln was no longer welcome in the Edwards home. And back in Kentucky, Mary's father objected vigorously to the match.

Mary was defiant. She would not be told whom to marry! But Lincoln was wounded by the Todd family's rejection. "One *d* is enough for God," he told a friend, "but the Todds need two."

Early in 1841 Lincoln broke off the engagement. He had known bouts of depression before, but now he plunged into the worst emotional crisis of his life. For a week, he refused to leave his room. People around town said that he had thrown "two cat fits and a duck fit." He had gone "crazy for a week or two." To his law partner Stuart, who was serving a term in Congress, Lincoln wrote: "I am the most miserable man living. If what I feel were equally distributed to the whole human family, there would not be one cheerful face on earth."

Fifteen months passed before friends arranged a secret meeting between Lincoln and Mary. When they saw each other again, they knew that they wanted to resume their courtship. On November 4, 1842, they told Elizabeth and Ninian that they intended to be married.

The wedding took place that evening in the Edwards parlor before a few close friends. Afterwards, the newlyweds climbed into a carriage and rode off through the rain to their first home—a furnished room in the Globe Tavern, where they paid four dollars a month for board and lodging. It was the best Lincoln could afford. A few days later he wrote to a friend: "Nothing new here, except my marrying, which to me is a matter of profound wonder."

As was the custom in those proper Victorian days, Lincoln called his bride Mary, while she addressed him as Mr. Lincoln. But this soon changed to Mother and Father. Their first child, named Robert Todd after Mary's father, was born at the Globe Tavern nine months after their wedding. A few months later, with financial help from Mary's father, the Lincolns bought a comfortable house where they would live for the next seventeen years. Three more sons were born in that house—Eddie in 1846, Willie in 1850, and Thomas or Tad in 1853.

Lincoln's career flourished. After working as a junior partner with John Todd Stuart and later with Stephen T. Logan, he opened

THE PEOPLE OF THE STATE OF ILLINOIS.

To any Minister of the Gospel, or other authorised Person---GREETING.

THESE are to License and permit you to join in the holy bands of Matrimony *Abraham Lincoln* and *Mary Todd* of the County of Sangamon and State of Illinois, and for so doing, this shall be your sufficient warrant.

Given under my hand and seal of office, at Springfield, in said County this 4 day of *Novmbr* 1842

A. N. Mathis ·Clerk.

Solemnized on the same 4th day of Nov. 1842 *Charles Dresser*

Marriage license of Abraham Lincoln and Mary Todd, dated November 4, 1842. They were married that evening.

Above: *Purchased for fifteen hundred dollars, this house at Eighth and Jackson streets in Springfield was the only home that Lincoln ever owned. In this 1860 photograph, Lincoln and his son Willie are standing on the terrace, just inside the picket fence.* Below: *The sitting room in Lincoln's home, as sketched for* Frank Leslie's Illustrated Newspaper *in 1860.*

his own law office. He invited talkative young William Herndon to join him as junior partner. Soon he was able to pay off the last of his New Salem debts. Meanwhile, he had his eye on a seat in Congress. In 1846, Lincoln won his party's nomination, and after a spirited campaign, he was elected by a large majority to the U.S. House of Representatives.

The following year he was off to Washington with Mary, four-year-old Robert, and the baby Eddie. They moved into a boardinghouse on Capitol Hill that catered to Whig politicians. But Mary found that she was bored and unhappy in Washington. After three months, she packed up and left with the boys to spend the rest of Lincoln's term with her family in Kentucky. "I hate to stay in this old room by myself," Lincoln wrote to her. "What did [Robert] and Eddie think of the little letters Father sent them? Don't let the blessed fellows forget father."

The major issues during Lincoln's term in Congress were the spread of slavery beyond the South, and the war between the United States and Mexico, which had broken out in 1846. By the time Lincoln took his seat in Congress, American troops had occupied Mexico City. The Mexican government was about to sign a peace treaty giving up more than two-fifths of its territory—including the present states of California, Nevada, and Utah, most of Arizona and New Mexico, and parts of Wyoming and Colorado.

Many Whigs had opposed the Mexican War. They accused President James Polk's Democratic administration of starting the conflict on purpose, in order to seize Mexican territory. Some Whigs charged that the war was a plot by Southern Democrats to grab vast new areas for the expansion of slavery.

Lincoln had criticized the war from the beginning. Soon after taking his seat in Congress, he introduced a series of resolutions attacking the Democrats' war policy, calling the war "immoral and unnecessary." Back home in Illinois, his antiwar stand did not go down well. Democratic newspapers ridiculed his "silly and imbecile" position, accusing him of a "treasonable assault" on the president. Illinois had wholeheartedly supported the war, and Lincoln's outspoken opposition almost wrecked his political career.

On the issue of slavery, his record was mixed. He supported a bill to prohibit slavery in any of the lands taken from Mexico. And he proposed a bill of his own to abolish slavery in the District of Columbia, but when the measure drew fire from both Whigs and Democrats, he dropped it. Aside from that, Lincoln took no active part in the growing antislavery movement in Congress.

His two-year term was a disappointment. When he returned home to Springfield, he was disappointed again. Lincoln had worked hard for the Whig party and its candidate Zachary Taylor, who was elected president in 1848. Afterward, he hoped to be rewarded with a government post as commissioner of the General Land Office. But the job went to someone else. With his political fortunes at a low ebb, Lincoln returned to full-time practice of the law.

Then he faced a personal tragedy. His boy Eddie, not yet four, fell gravely ill. After lingering for two months, the child died on February 1, 1850. Mary collapsed in shock. Robert, who was then six, would remember his mother's uncontrolled sobbing, the dark circles under his father's eyes, the house draped in black. Mary shut herself in her room and stayed there for weeks. Lincoln buried himself in his work.

Lincoln was now in his forties. He would usually walk the few blocks from his house to his law office in downtown Springfield, stopping along the way to greet friends and chat in his distinctive high-pitched voice. He walked with a slight stoop, head bent forward, stepping along firmly like a man following a plow.

The office of Lincoln & Herndon occupied two cluttered and unswept rooms on the second floor of a brick building across from the state capitol. Neither man was much for neatness, and people said that orange seeds sprouted in dusty office corners. Lincoln's favorite filing place for letters and papers was the lining of his high silk hat. When he was finished with documents, he stashed them away in mysterious places. After his death, Herndon found a bundle of papers marked: "When you can't find it anywhere else, look here."

When visitors called, Lincoln usually greeted them with one of his jokes or anecdotes. One morning a friend heard him tell the same story to three different callers, "and every time he laughed as heartily and enjoyed it as much as if it were a new story."

From their disorderly office, littered with letters, documents, journals, and books, Lincoln and Herndon handled more than a hundred cases a year. Lincoln became one of the most sought-after attorneys in the state. He took on all sorts of cases, ranging from disputes over runaway pigs to murder. And he represented all kinds of clients, from powerful corporations to penniless widows.

When he agreed to take on a client, he mastered every detail of the case before going to court. Once, during a lawsuit over patent rights, Lincoln wanted to show a jury the differences among various makes of mechanical reapers. Models of several reapers were brought into the courtroom. As he explained how each machine worked, he knelt down in order to point out the moving parts. Fascinated by his technical knowledge, the jurors left their seats, came over, and got down on their knees beside him.

Lincoln was at his best when addressing a jury. His speeches

William H. Herndon,
Lincoln's law partner
from 1844 to 1865.

were seasoned with wit and humor, and he could boil down the most complex issue to its simplest terms. Lincoln was shrewd, but he also had his superstitions. When selecting a jury, he would favor fat men (because they were jolly and easily swayed, he believed) and reject men with high foreheads (because they had already made up their minds).

In his most famous murder trial, Lincoln defended Duff Armstrong, the son of his old New Salem chum, Jack Armstrong. Duff and another man had been charged with attacking James Metzger during a drunken brawl. Metzger died three days later. The prosecution's star witness, Charles Allen, testified that he had seen Duff strike Metzger on the head with a slingshot. He had seen everything clearly, Allen testified, because a full moon was shining directly overhead.

When Lincoln rose to cross-examine the witness, he hooked his thumbs under his suspender straps and asked Allen to repeat his story. Now, was Allen sure about the moon being overhead? Allen was sure. Lincoln nodded and stroked his chin. Then he reached into his pocket, pulled out a copy of the 1857 almanac, flipped through the pages, and read aloud to the jury. At the time of the brawl, the moon wasn't directly overhead. It was low in the sky, about an hour away from setting. The jury quickly found Duff Armstrong not guilty.

Lincoln spent much of his time traveling through the Eighth Judicial Circuit, which sprawled across fourteen Illinois counties. Every spring, and again in the fall, the presiding judge left his Springfield headquarters to make a swing around the circuit, holding court for a few days in each county seat. Lincoln and other Springfield lawyers went along to try cases in remote prairie courthouses.

For six months a year, Lincoln rode from town to town along empty trails in an old horse-drawn rig, his legal papers and a change of clothing in his carpetbag. Lodging was primitive. Lawyers slept two to a bed, with three or four beds to a room in crude country inns. Criminals and judges often ate at the same table. Sometimes, Lincoln had just a few minutes to confer with a client before going to trial.

But he didn't mind the hardships. Life on the circuit offered a chance to meet all sorts of people, to sit by a roaring tavern fire in the evening, swapping stories and rehashing the day in court. And the long days of travel across the silent prairie gave him time to be alone with his thoughts, away from family interruptions. Out on the circuit he seemed "as happy as *he* could be," said a friend, "and happy no other place."

He was earning a substantial income now, but his rural habits stayed with him. Neighbors would remember Lincoln milking the

Lincoln at the age of forty-eight. "The picture . . . is, I think, a very true one; though my wife, and many others, do not," Lincoln wrote. "My impression is that their objection arises from the disordered condition of the hair."

family cow in the carriage shed before breakfast, grooming his horse in the backyard, chopping firewood by moonlight. On quiet family evenings he loved to sprawl on the parlor floor, reading his newspapers or roughhousing with Willie and Tad and their yellow dog, Fido.

Mary had a strong sense of propriety, and her husband's homespun manners riled her. She was annoyed when he answered the front door in his shirtsleeves, greeted guests in shabby carpet slippers, or littered the parlor with papers and books. When Mary lost her temper, the neighbors would hear her furious explosions of anger. Lincoln would simply walk out of the house, giving her time to calm down.

She wasn't easy to live with, but neither was Lincoln. His untidiness followed him home from the office. He cared little for the social niceties that were so important to his wife. He was absentminded, perpetually late for meals. He was away from home for weeks at a time, leaving Mary alone with a big house to run and children to care for. And he was moody, lapsing into long brooding silences. Like other couples, the Lincolns fought. But they always made up, and the love between them endured. If Mary scolded her husband for his failings, it was because she was so fiercely proud of his abilities.

They adored their boys, denied them nothing, and seldom disciplined them. Lincoln liked to take Willie and Tad to the office when he worked on Sundays. Their wild behavior infuriated his partner. "The boys were absolutely unrestrained in their amusement," Herndon complained. "If they pulled down all the books from the shelves, bent the points of all the pens, overturned the spittoon, it never disturbed the serenity of their father's good nature. I have felt many and many a time that I wanted to wring the necks of those little brats and pitch them out of the windows."

Mary Lincoln with her sons Willie (left) and Tad (right) in 1860.

But as far as Lincoln was concerned, his boys could do no wrong. "Mr. Lincoln . . . was very exceedingly indulgent to his children," Mary remarked. "He always said: 'It is my pleasure that my children are free, happy, and unrestrained by parental tyranny. Love is the chain whereby to bind a child to its parents.'"

Wanted poster for a runaway slave.

FOUR

Half Slave and Half Free

"If slavery is not wrong, nothing is wrong. I cannot remember when I did not so think, and feel."

When Lincoln took his seat in Congress in 1847, Washington was a sprawling town of 34,000 people, including several thousand slaves. From the windows of the Capitol, Lincoln could see crowded slave pens where manacled blacks waited to be shipped south.

Southern planters had built a cotton kingdom on the shoulders of enslaved blacks, and they meant to preserve their way of life. White Southerners claimed a "sacred" right to own Negroes as slaves. Slavery was a blessing for blacks and whites alike, they said, "a good—a positive good," according to Senator John C. Calhoun of South Carolina.

Slave uprisings and rebellions had resulted in tough measures to control blacks and silence white critics of slavery. Throughout the South, antislavery writings and societies were suppressed or banned.

Slavery had never prospered in the North and had been out-
lawed there. Some Northerners wanted to abolish slavery everywhere in the land, but abolitionists were still a small and
embattled minority. Most people in the North were willing to
leave slavery alone, as long as it was confined to the South.

While the North was free soil, it was hardly a paradise for
blacks. Racial prejudice was a fact of everyday life. Most Yankee
states had enacted strict "black laws." In Illinois, Lincoln's home
state, blacks paid taxes but could not vote, hold political office,
serve on juries, testify in court, or attend schools. They had a hard
time finding jobs. Often they sold themselves as "indentures" for
a period of twenty years—a form of voluntary slavery—just to eat
and have a place to live.

Even in northern Illinois, where antislavery feelings ran strong,
whites feared that emancipation of the slaves would send thousands of jobless blacks swarming into the North. Abolitionists
were considered dangerous fanatics in Illinois. Lincoln knew that
to be branded an abolitionist in his home state would be political
suicide.

Early in his career, Lincoln made few public statements about
slavery. But he did take a stand. As a twenty-eight-year-old state
legislator, he recorded his belief that slavery was "founded on both
injustice and bad policy." Ten years later, as a congressman, he
voted with his party to stop the spread of slavery, and he introduced his bill to outlaw slavery in the nation's capital. But he did
not become an antislavery crusader. For the most part, he sat silently in the background as Congress rang with angry debates over
slavery's future.

Lincoln always said that he hated slavery. He claimed he hated
it as much as any abolitionist, but he feared that efforts to force
abolition on the South would only lead to violence. He felt that

*Slave market in Atlanta. The slaves were held in pens until they were
auctioned off.*

Congress had no power to interfere with slavery in states where it already existed.

He wanted to see slavery done away with altogether, but that would take time, he believed. He hoped it could be legislated out of existence, with some sort of compensation given to the slaveholders in exchange for their property. As long as Congress kept slavery from spreading, Lincoln felt certain that it would gradually die a "natural death."

When his congressional term ended in 1849, Lincoln decided to withdraw from public life. For the next five years he concentrated on his law practice and stayed out of politics. As he traveled the Illinois circuit, arguing cases in country courthouses, slavery was becoming an explosive issue that threatened to tear the nation apart.

Vast new territories were opening up in the West, bringing the North and South into conflict. Each section wanted to control the western territories. The South needed new lands for the large-scale cultivation of cotton and other crops with slave labor. The North demanded that the western territories be reserved for the free labor of independent farmers and workers. Meanwhile, as the territories reached statehood and gained votes in Congress, they would hold the balance of political power in Washington. The admission of each new state raised a crucial question: Would it enter the Union as a free state or a slave state?

So far, Congress had managed to hold the country together through a series of uneasy compromises, such as the Missouri Compromise of 1820. These agreements permitted slavery in some western territories and barred it in others. But attitudes were hardening. Growing numbers of Northerners had come to regard slavery as a moral evil, an issue that could no longer be avoided. Southerners, meanwhile, were more determined than ever to protect their way of life.

Five generations of a slave family on a South Carolina plantation.

The issue came to a head in 1854, when Congress passed the bitterly debated Kansas-Nebraska Act. Under the Missouri Compromise, the region that included the territories of Kansas and Nebraska had been declared off-limits to slavery. Under the new Act, however, the future of slavery in those territories would be determined by the people who settled there. They would decide for themselves whether to enter the Union as free states or slave states.

The Kansas-Nebraska Act had been introduced by Lincoln's old political rival, Stephen Douglas, now a U.S. Senator from Illinois. Douglas's policy of "popular sovereignty" caused a storm of protest in the North. By opening new territories to slavery, his measure overturned the Missouri Compromise, which had held slavery in check. With the passage of Douglas's Act, Lincoln ended his long political silence. "I was losing interest in politics," he said, "when the repeal of the Missouri Compromise aroused me again."

He was "thunderstruck and stunned," aroused as he had "never been before." Douglas and his followers had opened the gates for slavery to expand and grow and establish itself permanently. Now it would never die the "natural death" Lincoln had expected. He felt compelled to speak out. For the first time in five years he neglected his law practice. He traveled across Illinois, campaigning for antislavery Whig candidates and speaking in reply to Senator Douglas, who had returned home to defend his policies.

Lincoln told his audiences that slavery was a "monstrous injustice." It was a "cancer" threatening to grow out of control "in a nation originally dedicated to the inalienable rights of man." And it was not only wrong, it threatened the rights of everyone. If slavery was permitted to spread, free white workers would be forced to compete for a living with enslaved blacks. In the end, slavery

135,000 SETS, 270,000 VOLUMES SOLD.

UNCLE TOM'S CABIN

FOR SALE HERE.

AN EDITION FOR THE MILLION, COMPLETE IN 1 Vol., PRICE 37 1-2 CENTS.

" " IN GERMAN, IN 1 Vol., PRICE 50 CENTS.

" " IN 2 Vols., CLOTH, 6 PLATES, PRICE $1.50.

SUPERB ILLUSTRATED EDITION, IN 1 Vol., WITH 153 ENGRAVINGS,

PRICES FROM $2.50 TO $5.00.

The Greatest Book of the Age.

Published as a book in 1852, Uncle Tom's Cabin *became an international best seller that for hundreds of thousands of readers dramatized the horrors of slavery.*

Harriet Beecher Stowe, author of Uncle Tom's Cabin.

would undermine the very foundations of democracy. "As I would not be a slave, so I would not be a master," Lincoln declared. "This expresses my idea of democracy. Whatever differs from this, to the extent of the difference, is not democracy."

He had been studying the history of the nation, pondering the words and ideals of the Founding Fathers. He believed that the cornerstone of the American experiment in democracy was the Declaration of Independence, which states that "all men are created equal," and that all are entitled to "Life, Liberty, and the pursuit of Happiness." Lincoln took this declaration personally. It meant that every poor man's son deserved the opportunities for advancement he had enjoyed. He felt that the Declaration of Independence expressed the highest political truths in history, and that blacks and whites alike were entitled to the rights it spelled out.

Although Lincoln was determined to oppose the spread of slavery, he admitted that he didn't know what to do about those states where slavery was already established, where it was protected by a complex web of state and national laws. "I have no prejudice against the Southern people," he said. "They are just what we would be in their situation. If slavery did not now exist amongst them, they would not introduce it. If it did now exist amongst us, we should not instantly give it up. . . . I surely will not blame them for not doing what I should not know how to do myself. If all earthly power were given me, I should not know what to do, as to the existing institution."

By 1856, open warfare had broken out in Kansas. Antislavery Northerners and proslavery Southerners had both recruited settlers to move into the territory. "Bleeding Kansas" became a battleground of rigged elections, burnings, lynchings, and assassinations as the rival forces fought for control of the territory.

Violence reached even to the floor of Congress. After delivering an impassioned anti-Southern speech on "The Crime Against Kansas," Senator Charles Sumner of Massachusetts was beaten with a cane and almost killed by Congressman Preston Brooks of South Carolina.

Then the U.S. Supreme Court handed down a decision that shocked antislavery forces everywhere. In 1857, the court ruled in the *Dred Scott* case that Congress had no power to prohibit slavery in any of the nation's territories, because that would violate property rights guaranteed by the Constitution. Scott was a slave who sued for his freedom on grounds that his master had twice taken him onto free soil in the North. The court declared that as a black man, Scott was not and never had been a citizen. He was not entitled to the rights spelled out by the Declaration of Independence. Slaves were private property, the court said, and Congress could not pass laws depriving white citizens of "the right of property in a slave."

The *Dred Scott* decision was a stunning setback for the opponents of slavery. But it also helped mobilize antislavery opinion. Lincoln spent two weeks studying the decision so he could prepare an argument against it. Speaking in Springfield, he pointed to the "plain unmistakable language" of the Declaration of Independence. When its authors declared that all men have equal rights, "This they said, and this they meant," Lincoln argued. He urged respect for the courts, but he added: "We think the *Dred Scott* decision is erroneous. We know the court that made it has often overruled its own decisions, and we shall do what we can to have it overrule this."

By now, Lincoln had become a leading antislavery spokesman in Illinois. And he had switched his political allegiance. Since entering politics he had been a Whig, but the Whigs had not been able to unite in opposition to slavery, and now the party was splin-

*Charles Sumner,
the ardent antislavery
senator from Massachusetts.*

*A newspaper drawing shows Representative Preston Brooks attacking
Senator Charles Sumner on the Senate floor.*

tered and dying. Thousands of Whigs had gone over to the Republicans, a new party founded in 1854 to oppose the spread of slavery. Lincoln remained loyal to the Whigs until 1856, when he made up his mind to leave his "mummy of a party" and join the Republicans himself.

He wanted to be in office again so he could influence public policy, and this time he was after Stephen Douglas's Senate seat. The two men had been rivals for twenty years now. Douglas had risen to national prominence. He had been a judge of the Illinois Supreme Court, a congressman and a senator, an outstanding leader of the Democratic party. Lincoln's political career had floundered after his solitary term in Congress. "With *me*, the race of ambition has been a failure—a flat failure," he remarked. "With *him* [Douglas] it has been one of splendid success. His name fills the nation and is not unknown, even, in foreign lands."

Lincoln had made an unsuccessful bid for the Senate as a Whig, in 1855. As a Republican he tried again, and in 1858 he won his new party's nomination. He launched his campaign on a sweltering June evening with a rousing speech before twelve hundred shirt-sleeved delegates at the state Republican convention in Springfield.

Where was the nation headed? Lincoln asked them. More than four years had passed since the passage of the Kansas-Nebraska Act, yet agitation over slavery had not ceased. "In my opinion," he sang out, "it *will* not cease, until a *crisis* shall have been reached, and passed.

"A house divided against itself cannot stand.

"I believe this government cannot endure, permanently half *slave* and half *free*.

"I do not expect the Union to be *dissolved*—I do not expect the house to *fall*—but I *do* expect it will cease to be divided.

"It will become *all* one thing, or *all* the other."

Lincoln warned that the opponents of slavery must stop its westward expansion. They must put slavery back on the "course of ultimate extinction." Otherwise slavery would spread its grip across the entire nation, "till it shall become lawful in *all* the States, *old* as well as *new—North* as well as *South.*"

There could be no fair fight between slavery and freedom, because one was morally wrong and the other morally right. Senator Douglas and the Democrats did not care about the advance of slavery, said Lincoln. The Republicans did care. The issue facing the country was the spread of slavery across the nation and into the future.

Some Republicans felt that the speech was too extreme, too much "ahead of its time." But most of the delegates in Lincoln's audience cheered him on. It was the strongest statement he had ever made about slavery. And it set the stage for his dramatic confrontation with Stephen Douglas.

The campaign between them during the summer of 1858 was to capture the attention of the entire nation. In July, Lincoln challenged Douglas to a series of public debates. Douglas accepted the challenge, agreeing to seven three-hour debates in small Illinois towns.

At least twelve thousand people were on hand for the first debate at Ottawa on August 21. More than fifteen thousand showed up at Freeport a week later, even though it rained. At every stop, people came from miles around in wagons and buggies, on horseback and on foot, to see and hear the candidates and decide who was the better man. Town squares were festooned with banners and flags. Peddlers hawked Lincoln and Douglas badges, bands played, cannons roared, and marshals on horseback tried to maintain order among huge crowds as the candidates arrived in town.

Douglas traveled in high style, riding from town to town in a private railroad car, sipping brandy and smoking cigars, sur-

With his opponent, Douglas, seated to his right, Lincoln addresses the crowd at Charleston, Illinois, on September 18, 1858. Lincoln and Douglas held seven debates, each lasting three hours. Painting by Robert Marshall Root.

rounded by friends and advisors and accompanied by his beautiful wife. Lincoln traveled more modestly, as an ordinary passenger on the regular trains. Mary stayed home with Willie and Tad. She heard her husband speak only once, at the final debate in Alton.

Newspaper reporters trailed the candidates, taking down their speeches in shorthand and telegraphing stories to their newspapers back east. What the debators said in remote Illinois towns could be read the next day in Boston or Atlanta.

The striking contrast between Douglas and Lincoln—The Little Giant and Long Abe, as reporters called them—added color and excitement to the contests. Douglas was Lincoln's opposite in every way. Barely five feet four inches tall, he had a huge round head planted on massive shoulders, a booming voice, and an ag-

Left: *Five feet four—Senator Stephen A. Douglas, nicknamed The Little Giant. His booming voice and confident manner made up for his small stature.*
Right: *Six feet four—A. Lincoln, also known as Long Abe or The Tall Sucker. His eventual victory over Douglas earned him another nickname—The Giant Killer.*

gressive, self-confident manner. He appeared on the speakers' platform dressed "plantation style"—a navy coat and light trousers, a ruffled shirt, a wide-brimmed felt hat. Lincoln, tall and gangly, seemed plain in his rumpled suit, carrying his notes and speeches in an old carpetbag, sitting on the platform with his bony knees jutting into the air.

The give and take between them held audiences spellbound. Douglas defended his doctrine of popular sovereignty. The nation *could* endure half slave and half free, he argued. Each state had the right to decide for itself the question of slavery.

Lincoln replied that popular sovereignty was just a smoke screen to allow the spread of slavery. The country had endured for decades half slave and half free only because most people believed that slavery would die out. Besides, slavery wasn't just a matter of states' rights. It was a moral issue that affected the whole country. "This government was instituted to secure the blessings of freedom," said Lincoln. "Slavery is an unqualified evil to the Negro, to the white man, to the soil, and to the State."

Douglas argued that the constitutional guarantee of equality applied only to white citizens, not to blacks. The Supreme Court had ruled that blacks weren't citizens at all. "I am opposed to Negro equality," said Douglas. "I believe this government was made by the white man for the white man to be administered by the white man."

Douglas pressed the issue of white supremacy. Was Lincoln in favor of Negro equality? Did he advocate a mixing of the races? In Illinois, where many voters opposed equal rights for blacks, these were touchy questions. Across the state, Douglas kept race-baiting Lincoln, warning white crowds that he was a "Black Republican" who wanted to liberate the slaves so they could stampede into Illinois to work, vote, and marry with white people.

Lincoln complained bitterly that Douglas was twisting and distorting the issue through a "fantastic arrangement of words, by which a man can prove a horse chestnut to be a chestnut horse." The issue was not the social or political equality of the races, he protested defensively. He had never advocated that Negroes should be voters or office holders, or that they should marry whites. The real issue was whether slavery would spread and become permanent in America, or whether it would be confined to the South and allowed to die out gradually.

Lincoln appealed to the voters to "discard all this quibbling about this man and the other man—this race and that race and the other race as being inferior." And he added: "There is no reason in the world why the Negro is not entitled to all the natural rights enumerated in the Declaration of Independence, the right to life, liberty, and the pursuit of happiness. I hold that he is as much entitled to these as the white man."

At the time, senators were elected by state legislatures, not by popular vote. When the returns came in, the Republicans had not won enough seats in the legislature to send Lincoln to the Senate. Douglas was reelected by a narrow margin. "The fight must go on," Lincoln told a friend. "The cause of civil liberty must not be surrendered at the end of one or even one hundred defeats." Even so, the defeat hurt. "I feel like the boy who stumped his toe," he said. "I am too big to cry and too badly hurt to laugh."

Lincoln lost the election, but the debates had catapulted him to national prominence. He continued to speak out on the issues in Illinois and throughout the North, and by 1860, he was being mentioned as a possible candidate for president. At first he doubted that he could win. "I must, in all candor, say I do not think myself fit for the presidency," he told an Illinois newspaper editor. But powerful Republican leaders felt that Lincoln had a good chance to carry the party banner to victory. As they began to work for his nomination, he did not interfere. "The taste *is* in my mouth a little," he admitted.

When Illinois Republicans held their state convention on May 9, 1860, Lincoln was chosen unanimously as their favorite-son candidate. The cheering delegates lifted his long frame overhead and passed him hand-by-hand down to the speaker's platform.

A week later, the national convention of the Republican party met in Chicago. Several prominent Republicans were competing for the presidency, and Lincoln was not the first choice of many delegates. But he was acceptable to all factions of the party, and after some backstage maneuvering, he was nominated on the third ballot. He had spent the day quietly down in Springfield, waiting for news from the convention, and passing the time playing handball.

Meanwhile, the Democratic party had split in two. Northern Democrats meeting in Baltimore nominated Stephen Douglas for president. Southern Democrats, unwilling to accept any Northerner, held their own convention in Richmond, Virginia, and nominated John C. Breckinridge of Kentucky. Another group, the Constitutional Union party, also entered the contest with John Bell of Tennessee as their candidate.

It wasn't customary in those days for a Presidential candidate to campaign on his own behalf. Lincoln didn't even leave Springfield until after Election Day. But his supporters carried on a spirited campaign, playing up Lincoln's humble background. At Republican rallies and parades all over the North, he was hailed as Honest Abe, the homespun rail-splitter from Illinois, a man of the people who was born in a log cabin and was headed for the White House.

Shortly before the election, Lincoln received a letter from Grace

Bedell, an eleven-year-old girl in Westfield, New York, suggesting that he grow a beard. ". . . you would look a great deal better for your face is so thin," she wrote. "All the ladies like whiskers and they would tease their husbands to vote for you." As he waited for the nation to vote, Lincoln took her advice.

On Election Day—November 6, 1860—Lincoln waited in the Springfield telegraph office until he was certain of victory. Then he went out into the streets of Springfield to be greeted by fireworks and torchlight parades. Mary joined him, radiant and beaming, at a Republican Ladies' supper that evening. A guest reported that the women paid "solicitous attention" to the president-elect, fetching him coffee, serving him sandwiches, and serenading him with "vigorous Republican choruses."

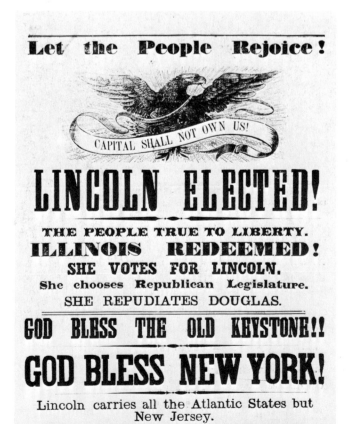

Republican victory poster, 1860.

A crowd of well-wishers gathers in front of Lincoln's home to celebrate his nomination as Republican candidate for president in 1860. Lincoln is standing to the right of the doorway in a white summer suit.

Lincoln received 1,866,000 votes and carried every Northern state. Douglas had 1,377,000 votes, and Breckinridge, the candidate of the Southern Democrats, 850,000 votes. The North had swept Lincoln into office. In the South, his name hadn't even appeared on the ballot.

Douglas had warned that a Republican victory would bring on "a war of sections, a war of the North against the South, of the free states against the slave states—a war of extermination." Southern leaders were saying that they would never accept this

Lincoln's last beardless portrait, August 13, 1860.

The president-elect sprouts whiskers, November 25, 1860.

"Black Republican" as president. They were already threatening to withdraw from the Union and form an independent slave nation. An Atlanta newspaper declared: "Let the consequences be what they may . . . the South will never submit to such humiliation and degradation as the inauguration of Abraham Lincoln."

In December—three months before Lincoln took his oath of office—South Carolina led the way. The state announced that it had seceded from the Union. It was now a sovereign nation, dedicated to the preservation of slavery.

Lincoln with a full beard, January 13, 1861. "Old Abe is . . . puttin' on (h)airs!" a newspaper joked.

February 9, 1861. Two days later, Lincoln left for Washington to become the first bearded president of the United States.

Thousands of people gather in front of the unfinished U.S. Capitol to witness Lincoln's inauguration on March 4, 1861. Note the fashionable stovepipe hats scattered through the crowd.

✑ FIVE ✑
Emancipation

"If my name ever goes into history, it will be for this act."

On Inauguration Day—March 4, 1861—Washington looked like an armed camp. Cavalry and artillery had been clattering through the streets all morning. Troops were everywhere. Rumors of assassination plots, of Southern plans to seize the capital and prevent the inauguration, had put the army on the alert.

Shortly after noon, the carriage bearing President James Buchanan and President-elect Abraham Lincoln bounced over the cobblestones of Pennsylvania Avenue, heading for Capitol Hill. Infantrymen lined the parade route. Army sharpshooters crouched on nearby rooftops. Soldiers surrounded the Capitol building, and plainclothes detectives mingled with the crowds. On a hill overlooking the Capitol, artillerymen manned a line of howitzers and watched for trouble.

A long covered passageway had been built to protect the presidential party on its way to the speaker's platform in front of the Capitol. More than three hundred dignitaries crowded the platform, waiting to witness the swearing-in ceremony. Among them was Stephen Douglas, who had pledged to support the new administration.

Lincoln was visibly nervous. He was wearing a new black suit and sporting a neatly clipped beard. He held his silk stovepipe hat in one hand, a gold-headed cane in the other. He put the cane in a corner, then looked around, trying to find a place for the hat. Stephen Douglas smiled and took the hat from him.

Lincoln unrolled the manuscript of his inaugural address. He put on his steel-rimmed spectacles and faced the sunlit crowd below. Thousands of people jammed the broad square in front of the Capitol, waiting to hear the new president speak.

Four months had passed since Lincoln's election in November. During that time, seven Southern states had left the Union, and four more were about to join them. In February, Senator Jefferson Davis of Mississippi had been sworn in as president of the Confederate States of America. Now, with the Union collapsing, the defiant South was preparing for war.

Congressional leaders had tried to find a compromise plan that would hold the Union together. But the Southerners would not budge from their demands. They wanted slavery to be guaranteed not only in the South, but wherever else it might spread—to the western territories, and perhaps even to Central America and the Caribbean. By the time Lincoln left Springfield for Washington on the eve of his fifty-second birthday, all attempts at compromise had failed.

He traveled east on a special presidential train, stopping at dozens of cities, towns, and villages along the route. Thousands of Americans had a chance to see and hear their elected leader for

The new president.

*The First Lady
in the gown she wore
to the inauguration ball.*

the first time. "Last night I saw the new president," one man reported. "He is a clever man, *and not so bad looking as they say,* while he is no great beauty. He is tall . . . has a commanding figure, bows pretty well, is not stiff, has a pleasant face, is amiable and *determined.*"

At Philadelphia, the presidential train was met by detectives who had uncovered evidence of an assassination plot, a plan to murder Lincoln as he traveled through Baltimore the next day. He was persuaded to switch trains and travel secretly through the night to Washington, accompanied by armed guards. When his night train passed through Baltimore at 3:30 A.M., Lincoln was safely hidden in a sleeping berth. He arrived in Washington at dawn, unnoticed and unannounced.

Word of Lincoln's secret night ride spread fast. Opposition newspapers ridiculed the president-elect, calling his escape from Baltimore "the flight of Abraham." The abuse became nasty. Hostile editors and politicians snickered at "this backwoods President" and his "boorish" wife. They taunted Lincoln as a hick with a high-pitched voice and a Kentucky twang, an ugly "gorilla" and "baboon." Lincoln shrugged off the insults as a hazard of his job, but Mary was mortified.

He was still living under this cloud when he stood in front of the Capitol on Inauguration Day, ready to take his oath of office as the sixteenth president of the United States. In his speech, he appealed to the people of the South, assuring them again that he would not tamper with slavery in their states:

"In *your* hands, my dissatisfied countrymen, and not in *mine,* is the momentous issue of civil war. The government will not assail *you.* You can have no conflict, without being yourselves the aggressors. *You* have no oath registered in Heaven to destroy the government, while *I* shall have the most solemn one to 'preserve, protect and defend' it."

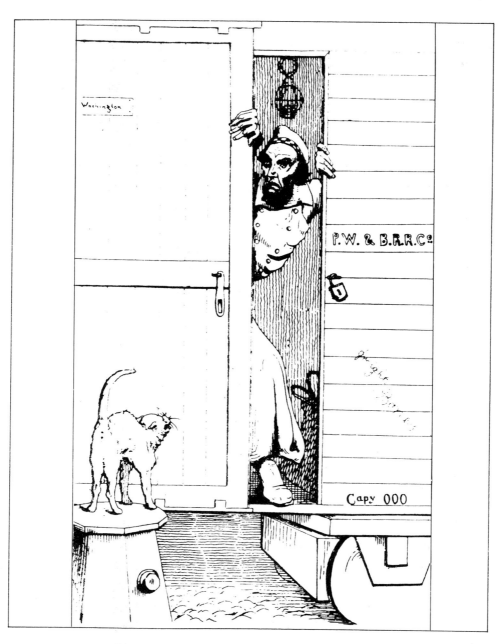

A Baltimore newspaper cartoon ridicules Lincoln's secret arrival in Washington.

Lincoln wanted to believe that the Union could be saved without bloodshed. But that hope was about to vanish. Less than two weeks after his inauguration, he faced his first crisis. Fort Sumter, at the entrance to Charleston harbor in South Carolina, still flew the Union flag. The state's governor was demanding that the fort be given up.

On March 15, Lincoln learned that Sumter was running out of supplies. While the fort was not of great military value, the president had pledged to defend federal property in the South. Sumter had become a symbol of Northern determination, and Lincoln had to make a decision. If he sent supplies, he risked an armed attack and war. If he didn't, the fort could not hold out for long.

He consulted with his military staff and members of his cabinet, but they could not agree on what should be done. Lincoln himself was uncertain. All the troubles and anxieties of his life, he later said, were nothing compared to the weeks that followed.

Finally the president acted. On April 6 he notified the South Carolina governor that a supply fleet was about to sail for Charleston. As the Union ships approached the city on the morning of April 12, rebel cannons ringing the harbor opened fire on Fort Sumter.

The American Civil War had begun.

On April 14, Lincoln heard that the fort had surrendered after a blistering thirty-six-hour bombardment. That day he issued a proclamation calling for 75,000 volunteers for enlistments of ninety days, which seemed long enough. Surely the rebellion would be put down by then.

Stephen Douglas called at the White House and again offered his support. Despite his disagreements with Lincoln, he wanted to preserve the Union. Then Douglas left for Illinois to denounce the rebels and rally Northern Democrats to the Union cause. A month later he was dead of typhoid fever at the age of forty-eight.

The North mobilized. Troops poured into Washington, ready to defend the capital. Across the Potomac River, Virginia had joined the Confederacy. From his office windows, Lincoln could see rebel flags flying over buildings in Alexandria, Virginia.

Everyone in Washington believed that the war would end quickly. The North claimed the loyalty of twenty-three states with a population of 22 million. The eleven states of the Confederacy had about 9 million people, and nearly 4 million of them were slaves. The South was mainly agricultural. The North had factories to produce ammunition and guns, a network of railroads to transport troops, and a powerful navy that could blockade Southern ports.

But if the North had most of the industry and population, the South held a monopoly on military talent. Jefferson Davis, the Confederate president, was a professional soldier. And Southern-

Jefferson Davis, president of the Confederate States of America.

ers made up a high proportion of the country's skilled military commanders. Lincoln's biggest headache during the early years of the war would be to find competent generals who could lead the Union to victory.

By early summer, both sides were training large armies of volunteers, many of them inexperienced boys who could barely handle a rifle. Northern newspapers were calling for a massive drive against the Confederate capital in Richmond, Virginia. "On to Richmond!" became the popular rallying cry.

In July, Union forces under General Irwin McDowell marched into Virginia. McDowell had been ordered to capture the crucial railroad junction at Manassas, about twenty-five miles southwest of Washington. From there, he would sweep down to Richmond and crush the rebellion.

Word spread through Washington that McDowell would begin his attack on Sunday, July 21. That morning dozens of politicians and their wives, newspapermen, and other spectators drove down from Washington in buggies and carriages to watch their army defeat the rebels. None of these people had ever seen a battle, and they had little idea what to expect. They brought along picnic baskets, champagne, and opera glasses, camped on a hillside, and waited for the action to begin.

Lincoln waited anxiously in the White House. The first reports to reach him were confusing—the two armies had met at a muddy little creek called Bull Run. They were advancing and retreating in turn. Several hours later, Lincoln received word of a disaster. Union troops had broken ranks. McDowell's army had been routed.

The president stayed up all that night, listening to the stories of congressmen and other civilians who had fled in panic before the retreating troops. The Union army had fallen apart. Soldiers

Many recruits on both sides of the Civil War were scarcely more than boys. This is a portrait of Edwin Jennison, a Georgia private, killed in action at Malvern Hill on July 1, 1862.

Union forces are routed at the Battle of Bull Run—the first major engagement of the war.

and sightseers alike had stampeded back to Washington. As dawn broke, Lincoln stood at a White House window and watched his mud-splattered troops straggling back into the capital through the fog and rain.

Until now, Lincoln had turned for strategic advice to his general in chief, seventy-five-year-old Winfield Scott. Scott had proposed his famous "anaconda plan" to surround the South and squeeze it into submission—a blockade of the Southern coast and occupation of the Mississippi River. Lincoln felt that the plan didn't go far enough. He wanted his commanders to take the offensive wherever they could. After Bull Run, he resolved to tighten the naval blockade, call up more troops for longer enlistments, and launch three offensives at once—into Virginia, into Tennessee, and down the Mississippi.

He gave command of the Eastern armies to General George B. McClellan, a thirty-five-year-old veteran of the Mexican War. McClellan was vain, pompous, and opinionated, but Lincoln had faith in him. The president brushed off criticism of the general's rude behavior by saying, "Never mind. I will hold McClellan's stirrups if he will bring us victory."

McClellan trained his growing army with meticulous care, but as the months passed, he showed no signs of moving against the rebel forces massed in Virginia. "Don't let them hurry me, is all I ask," he said. When the first snows fell at the end of 1861, McClellan's troops were not yet ready for battle. On the western front, it was the same story. Union commanders built up their forces and drilled their men, but they weren't ready to fight.

Congress and the public were losing patience. Why weren't the generals fighting? Was Lincoln too inexperienced to handle his job? A Congressional committee began to investigate the conduct of the war. Generals were called in from the field to testify on Capitol Hill.

Lincoln, too, was tired of the delays. But he wasn't a military man himself, and he was reluctant to overrule his commanders. And he had other troubles besides—corruption in the War Department, angry disputes within his cabinet, and mounting criticism from Congress. Senator Benjamin F. Wade of Ohio called the Lincoln administration "blundering, cowardly, and inefficient."

By now, the president had serious misgivings about the professional soldiers who were running the war. He had collected a library of books on military strategy, and he studied them late into the night, just as he had once studied law and surveying. Attorney General Edward Bates had told Lincoln that it was his presidential

The Overdue Bill. A cartoon from the British magazine Punch *pokes fun at Lincoln's vow to end the rebellion quickly.*

duty to "command the commanders. . . . The nation requires it, and history will hold you responsible." Lincoln began to play an active role in the day-to-day conduct of the war, planning strategy and sometimes directing tactical maneuvers in the field.

He found relief from the pressures of the war during his private hours in the White House. Robert Lincoln was now studying at Harvard University, but eleven-year-old Willie and eight-year-old Tad lived with their parents in the executive mansion. They romped through the house, bursting into solemn conferences, playing tricks on cabinet members, making friends with the staff, and collecting a menagerie of pets, including a pony that they rode around the White House grounds, and a goat that slept on Tad's bed.

Robert Todd Lincoln, the Lincolns' eldest son, as a student at Harvard University in 1861.

Lincoln took the boys with him to visit troops camped along the Potomac. And he joined in their games, wrestling with his sons on the expensive Oriental carpets Mary had bought when she redecorated the White House. During the darkest moments of the war, Lincoln was able to throw off his fits of despair in the company of his two boys.

In February, 1862, both boys came down with fevers. Tad recovered, but Willie took a turn for the worse, tossing and turning through the night as his parents sat by his bedside, bathing his face and trying to comfort him. Willie died on February 20—the second son to be taken from the Lincolns. Mary was so overwhelmed with grief, she could not attend the funeral. For three months she refused to leave the White House. She would never fully recover from her emotional breakdown.

Lincoln plunged into the deepest gloom he had ever known. He had felt a special bond of understanding with Willie, and now he grieved as never before. Again and again, he shut himself in his room to weep alone.

As Willie lay dying, the pace of the war was quickening. Union armies had launched a broad offensive in the West, winning the first Northern victories of the war. By the spring of 1862, the North had captured New Orleans and was gaining control of the crucial Mississippi River. While the news was encouraging, the cost in human lives horrified everyone. During a single two-day battle at Shiloh Church in southern Tennessee, thirteen thousand Union soldiers had been killed or wounded.

On the Eastern front, General McClellan had finally led his huge army into Virginia. Instead of marching overland to Richmond, as Lincoln had urged, McClellan shipped his troops to the tip of the York Peninsula, landing seventy-five miles southeast of

Thomas ("Tad") Lincoln, the youngest son, in his colonel's uniform. Tad and Willie were the first presidential children to live in the White House.

William Wallace ("Willie") Lincoln. His death in the White House in 1862 plunged the Lincolns into profound sorrow. "He was too good for this earth," the president was heard to say. "It is hard, hard to have him die."

Richmond. Then he moved up the peninsula to attack the Confederate capital from the rear. Unfortunately, he advanced so slowly and cautiously, the rebels had plenty of time to muster their defenses.

In June, as McClellan paused outside Richmond, waiting to attack, rebel troops commanded by Robert E. Lee launched a surprise counter-offensive. During seven days of bitter fighting, McClellan was driven all the way back to the James River. His long-awaited campaign to take Richmond had been a bloody failure. More than twenty-three thousand of his troops were either dead, wounded, or missing.

Meanwhile, the rebels had been battering Union armies in Virginia's Shenandoah Valley. As the casualty lists piled up on his desk, Lincoln wondered if the war would ever end. In the all-important Eastern theatre, the North had yet to win a victory.

For months, Lincoln had been shuffling his generals around, trying to find field commanders he could count on and a reliable general in chief to direct the war effort. The elderly and ailing Winfield Scott had been persuaded to retire. McClellan had stepped in as supreme commander, but he had little talent for strategic planning. When he sailed with his army for Virginia, Lincoln decided to act as his own general in chief. Then he called on General Henry W. Halleck to fill the top military command post. But Halleck was another disappointment. He offered good advice, but he shrank from making decisions. Once again, Lincoln had to make them.

The toughest decision facing Lincoln, however, was the one he had to make about slavery. Early in the war, he was still willing to leave slavery alone in the South, if only he could restore the Union. Once the rebellion was crushed, slavery would be confined to the Southern states, where it would gradually die out. "We

Left: *Winfield ("Old Fuss and Feathers") Scott, Lincoln's first general in chief. Suffering from vertigo and other ailments, he retired in October 1861.*

Below left: *George B. ("Little Mac") McClellan, who replaced Scott as general in chief. Dismissed from his command for failing to launch an offensive, McClellan ran against Lincoln in the presidential election of 1864.*

Below right: *Henry W. ("Old Brains") Halleck, Lincoln's general in chief from 1862 to 1864. A capable administrator, he shrank from making decisions.*

didn't go into the war to put down slavery, but to put the flag back," Lincoln said. "To act differently at this moment would, I have no doubt, not only weaken our cause, but smack of bad faith."

Abolitionists were demanding that the president free the slaves at once, by means of a wartime proclamation. "Teach the rebels and traitors that the price they are to pay for the attempt to abolish this Government must be the abolition of slavery," said Frederick Douglass, the famous black editor and reformer. "Let the war cry be down with treason, and down with slavery, the cause of treason!"

But Lincoln hesitated. He was afraid to alienate the large numbers of Northerners who supported the Union but opposed emancipation. And he worried about the loyal, slaveholding border states—Kentucky, Missouri, Maryland, and Delaware—that had refused to join the Confederacy. Lincoln feared that emancipation might drive those states into the arms of the South.

Yet slavery was the issue that had divided the country, and the president was under mounting pressure to do something about it. At first he supported a voluntary plan that would free the slaves gradually and compensate their owners with money from the federal treasury. Emancipation would begin in the loyal border states and be extended into the South as the rebel states were conquered. Perhaps then the liberated slaves could be resettled in Africa or Central America.

Lincoln pleaded with the border-state congressmen to accept his plan, but they turned him down. They would not part with their slave property or willingly change their way of life. "Emancipation in the cotton states is simply an absurdity," said a Kentucky congressman. "There is not enough power in the world to compel it to be done."

Lincoln came to realize that if he wanted to attack slavery, he would have to act more boldly. A group of powerful Republican senators had been urging him to act. It was absurd, they argued, to fight the war without destroying the institution that had caused it. Slaves provided a vast pool of labor that was crucial to the South's war effort. If Lincoln freed the slaves, he could cripple the Confederacy and hasten the end of the war. If he did not free them, then the war would settle nothing. Even if the South agreed to return to the Union, it would start another war as soon as slavery was threatened again.

Besides, enslaved blacks were eager to throw off their shackles and fight for their own freedom. Thousands of slaves had already escaped from behind Southern lines. Thousands more were ready to enlist in the Union armies. "You need more men," Senator Charles Sumner told Lincoln, "not only at the North, but at the South, in the rear of the rebels. You need the slaves."

All along, Lincoln had questioned his authority as president to abolish slavery in those states where it was protected by law. His Republican advisors argued that in time of war, with the nation in peril, the president *did* have the power to outlaw slavery. He could do it in his capacity as commander in chief of the armed forces. Such an act would be justified as a necessary war measure, because it would weaken the enemy. If Lincoln really wanted to save the Union, Senator Sumner told him, he must act now. He must wipe out slavery.

The war had become an endless nightmare of bloodshed and bungling generals. Lincoln doubted if the Union could survive without bold and drastic measures. By the summer of 1862, he had worked out a plan that would hold the loyal slave states in the Union, while striking at the enemies of the Union.

On July 22, 1862, he revealed his plan to his cabinet. He had decided, he told them, that emancipation was "a military necessity, absolutely essential to the preservation of the Union." For that reason, he intended to issue a proclamation freeing all the slaves in rebel states that had not returned to the Union by January 1, 1863. The proclamation would be aimed at the Confederate South only. In the loyal border states, he would continue to push for gradual, compensated emancipation.

Some cabinet members warned that the country wasn't ready to accept emancipation. But most of them nodded their approval, and in any case, Lincoln had made up his mind. He did listen to the objection of William H. Seward, his secretary of state. If Lincoln published his proclamation now, Seward argued, when Union armies had just been defeated in Virginia, it would seem like an act of desperation, "the last shriek on our retreat." The president must wait until the Union had won a decisive military victory in the East. Then he could issue his proclamation from a position of strength. Lincoln agreed. For the time being, he filed the document away in his desk.

A month later, in the war's second battle at Bull Run, Union forces commanded by General John Pope suffered another humiliating defeat. "We are whipped again," Lincoln moaned. He feared now that the war was lost. Rebel troops under Robert E. Lee were driving north. Early in September, Lee invaded Maryland and advanced toward Pennsylvania.

Lincoln again turned to General George McClellan—Who else do I have? he asked—and ordered him to repel the invasion. The two armies met at Antietam Creek in Maryland on September 17 in the bloodiest single engagement of the war. Lee was forced to retreat back to Virginia. But McClellan, cautious as ever, held his position and failed to pursue the defeated rebel army. It wasn't the decisive victory Lincoln had hoped for, but it would have to do.

Because cameras required long exposures, Civil War photographers could not take clear action shots. This photograph, taken at Antietam by Mathew Brady in September 1862, is believed to be the only actual battle picture of the entire war.

Dead soldiers lie where they fell on the battlefield at Antietam.

On September 22, Lincoln read the final wording of his Emancipation Proclamation to his cabinet. If the rebels did not return to the Union by January 1, the president would free "thenceforward and forever" all the slaves everywhere in the Confederacy. Emancipation would become a Union war objective. As Union armies smashed their way into rebel territory, they would annihilate slavery once and for all.

The next day, the proclamation was released to the press. Throughout the North, opponents of slavery hailed the measure, and black people rejoiced. Frederick Douglass, the black abolitionist, had criticized Lincoln severely in the past. But he said now: "We shout for joy that we live to record this righteous decree."

When Lincoln delivered his annual message to Congress on December 1, he asked support for his program of military emancipation:

"Fellow citizens, *we* cannot escape history. We of this Congress and this administration, will be remembered in spite of ourselves. . . . In *giving* freedom to the *slave,* we *assure* freedom to the *free*—honorable alike in what we give, and what we preserve."

On New Year's Day, after a fitful night's sleep, Lincoln sat at his White House desk and put the finishing touches on his historic decree. From this day forward, all slaves in the rebel states were "forever free." Blacks who wished to could now enlist in the Union army and sail on Union ships. Several all-black regiments were formed immediately. By the end of the war, more than 180,000 blacks—a majority of them emancipated slaves—had volunteered for the Union forces. They manned military garrisons and served as front-line combat troops in every theatre of the war.

The traditional New Year's reception was held in the White House that morning. Mary appeared at an official gathering for the

Lincoln reads the Emancipation Proclamation to his cabinet. Engraving by Edward Herline.

first time since Willie's death, wearing garlands in her hair and a black shawl about her head.

During the reception, Lincoln slipped away and retired to his office with several cabinet members and other officials for the formal signing of the proclamation. He looked tired. He had been shaking hands all morning, and now his hand trembled as he picked up a gold pen to sign his name.

Ordinarily he signed "A. Lincoln." But today, as he put pen to paper, he carefully wrote out his full name. "If my name ever goes into history," he said then, "it will be for this act."

Union soldiers wait in their trenches during the siege of Petersburg, Virginia, 1865.

SIX

This Dreadful War

"When I think of the sacrifice yet to be offered and the hearts and homes yet to be made desolate before this dreadful war is over, my heart is like lead within me, and I feel at times like hiding in a deep darkness."

Many people rejoiced when Lincoln signed the Emancipation Proclamation. But many others denounced the president. The proclamation infuriated thousands of Northern Democrats who cared nothing about freeing the slaves. They had supported a war to save the Union as it was, with slavery intact, and they weren't willing to fight for black liberation.

From all over the North came cries that the president was a tyrant, an abolitionist dictator. Democratic newspapers called the proclamation unconstitutional, "A wicked, atrocious, and revolting deed." When Lincoln's critics demanded that he change his emancipation policy, he replied: "I am a slow walker, but I never walk backward."

Opposition to Lincoln's wartime policies was growing. Early in the war he had imposed measures to deal with the "enemy in the rear"—Northerners who sympathized with the South and threatened to sabotage the war effort. He had allowed army commanders to declare martial law in some areas. And he had suspended the right of *habeas corpus,* which meant that the army could arrest and jail suspected traitors without trial.

As if that weren't bad enough, the president had introduced a military draft to overcome manpower shortages. And now he was enlisting blacks in the armed forces, allowing them to carry guns and wear the Union uniform.

Antiwar feelings were boiling over. Early in 1863, Northern Democrats launched a peace movement to stop the war and bring the boys home. Calling themselves Peace Democrats, they demanded an immediate truce and a constitutional amendment that would guarantee slavery in the South. They attacked Lincoln's policies right down the line—the draft, the military arrests, the use of Negro troops, and above all, the Emancipation Proclamation.

Lincoln reminded his critics that thousands of black soldiers were now fighting and dying in the Union ranks: "You say you will not fight to free Negroes. Some of them seem willing to fight for you. . . . Why should they do anything for us, if we will do nothing for them? If they stake their lives for us, they must be prompted by the strongest motive—even the promise of freedom. And the promise being made, must be kept."

Republicans charged that the Peace Democrats were poisonous "Copperheads." They branded them disloyal, accused them of aiding the rebels and undermining the war effort. Lincoln took a firm stand. He authorized army officers to jail anyone who obstructed the draft or otherwise helped the rebellion. By the summer of 1863, more then thirteen thousand opponents of the war had been

Black infantrymen photographed at Fort Lincoln by Mathew Brady.

Pvt. Abraham Brown, 54th Massachusetts Regiment, 1863.

crowded into Northern prisons. When Lincoln was criticized for jailing a prominent Ohio Democrat who had denounced the draft, he snapped back, "Must I shoot a simple-minded soldier boy who deserts while I must not touch a hair of the wily agitator who induces him to desert?"

That summer, violent draft riots flared up in several Northern cities. In New York, a rampaging mob burned down the draft office, attacked the mayor's house, and surged into the city's Negro district, clubbing and whipping blacks to death, and killing policemen and other whites who tried to interfere. More than five hundred people had died before federal troops could restore order.

The governor of New York demanded that Lincoln suspend the draft and revoke the Emancipation Proclamation. Lincoln replied that he would never abandon emancipation. And the draft would continue, because the Union needed men to see the war through to victory. His secretary, John Hay, was impressed by how tough the president had become. "He will not be bullied," said Hay, "even by his friends."

Yet victory was nowhere in sight. For months the fighting had continued with a mounting death toll. Lincoln was still having bad luck with his generals. At Antietam, McClellan had stopped Lee's advance into Maryland, but he hadn't gone after the rebels. Instead, he dug in at Antietam, complaining about his lack of supplies and his footsore horses while the president tried to prod him into action. "McClellan has got the slows," Lincoln muttered. By the time McClellan finally started in pursuit of Lee, the rebels had crossed the Blue Ridge Mountains and reached safety in central Virginia. Lincoln's patience was exhausted. In November, 1862, he dismissed McClellan from his command, ending the cautious general's troubled military career.

McClellan was replaced by General Ambrose E. Burnside, who

*Lincoln confers with General George McClellan at Antietam,
October 3, 1862.*

promptly marched south into Virginia and lost twelve thousand men at Fredericksburg. Burnside was so humiliated, he asked to be relieved of his command.

His replacement was General "Fighting Joe" Hooker, who began to plan a new campaign against the rebel forces in Virginia. "My plans are perfect," Hooker announced, "and when I start to carry them out, may God have mercy on General Lee, for I shall have none." But Hooker, like Burnside, lasted for just one battle. Early in May, 1863, he went down to defeat at Chancellorsville, losing seventeen thousand men as Lee routed the demoralized Union troops.

Lee was determined to carry the war into the North. In June, his troops pushed northwards from Virginia, marched across Maryland, and invaded Pennsylvania, throwing the North into a panic. Lincoln had replaced Hooker with a new commander, General George Gordon Meade, who rushed his forces to Pennsylvania to stop the rebels. The two armies met on July 1 at the little country town of Gettysburg, where 170,000 troops clashed in the most spectacular battle of the war.

On July 4, after three days of fierce fighting, with more than fifty thousand casualties on both sides, Lee's broken and defeated army started back to Virginia. When news of the victory reached Lincoln, he ordered Meade to go after Lee and destroy his army once and for all. "Do not let the enemy escape," Lincoln cabled. But Meade hesitated, allowing Lee to move his retreating troops safely across the Potomac. "We had them within our grasp," the president wailed. "We had only to stretch forth our hands and they were ours."

Lincoln had not yet found the commander he needed. He feared now that the war would go on indefinitely. "What can I do with such generals as we have?" he asked. "Who among them is any better than Meade?"

Pickett's charge at Gettysburg, the bloodiest battle in American history.

Union and Confederate dead on the battlefield at Gettysburg.

Four months later, a ceremony was held at Gettysburg to dedicate a national cemetery for the soldiers who had died there. The main speaker was to be Edward Everett of Massachusetts, the most celebrated orator of the day. The president was asked to deliver "a few appropriate remarks" after Everett had finished.

Lincoln wanted to make a brief statement about the larger meaning of the war, which was now well into its third year. He started work on his speech in Washington, but it was not yet finished when he rode a special train to Gettysburg the day before the ceremony. After dinner that evening, he retired to his room to work on the speech again. He added the final touches after breakfast the next morning. He had written it out on two pieces of lined paper. There were about 270 words. "It is what I would call a short, short speech," he said.

That morning, wearing his familiar black suit and silk stove-pipe hat, Lincoln rode on horseback to the cemetery on the outskirts of Gettysburg, accompanied by politicians and other dignitaries, by brass bands and marching soldiers. The official party paraded across the battlefield, where dead horses still lay stiffly on their sides among scattered autumn leaves. A crowd of fifteen thousand had assembled in front of the speaker's platform, which faced the unfinished cemetery's temporary graves and the famous battlefield beyond.

Edward Everett spoke for two hours as many in the crowd grew restless and wandered off to explore the battleground. Finally it was Lincoln's turn. He rose from his seat, took two bits of paper from his pocket, put on his spectacles, and in his reedy voice said: "Four score and seven years ago our fathers brought forth upon this continent, a new nation, conceived in liberty, and dedicated to the proposition that all men are created equal."

A photographer in the crowd fiddled with his camera, preparing to take a picture of the president as he spoke. But before he could get the camera ready, the speech was finished.

Lincoln spoke for two minutes. Some of his listeners were disappointed. Opposition newspapers criticized the address as unworthy of the occasion, and some papers didn't mention it at all. Lincoln himself felt that the speech was a failure. He certainly didn't realize that the words he spoke at Gettysburg on the afternoon of November 19, 1863, would be remembered all over the world as an American classic more than a hundred years later.

The war was being fought, Lincoln had said, to preserve America's bold experiment in democracy. A new kind of government had been created by the Founding Fathers in 1776. It was based on the idea that all men have an equal right to liberty, that they can govern themselves by free elections. The war was a test to determine if such a government could endure. Thousands of men had fought and died at Gettysburg so that the nation and its idea of democracy might survive. Now it was up to the living to complete their unfinished work, to make sure that "those dead shall not have died in vain—that this nation under God shall have a new birth of freedom—and that the government of the people, by the people, for the people, shall not perish from the earth."

Worry and fatigue had become etched into the president's features. As the war dragged on, Lincoln could not forget that the conflict involved human lives. The entrance hall to the White House was always jammed with people who wanted to see him, and he saw them all, sitting in his office day after day as he listened to their pleas and complaints.

He found it difficult to sleep and was usually up at dawn, so he could work quietly in his office before breakfast. Afterwards he returned to his desk for another hour before opening his door to visitors. He would put them at ease with a joke or story, ask "What can I do for you?" and then lean forward to listen, stroking his chin or clasping his knee with his hands as they talked. His secretaries complained that he was wearing himself out. But Lincoln would not give up the "public opinion baths" that brought him face-to-face with the citizens who came to his office in an endless stream.

One visitor was the influential black leader, Frederick Douglass. While Douglass differed with Lincoln on many issues, he had come to respect the president and like him personally. The two men were to meet several times. "In all my interviews with Mr.

Four score and seven years ago our fathers brought forth upon this continent, a new nation, conceived in Liberty, and dedicated to the proposition that all men are created equal.

Now we are engaged in a great civil war, testing whether that nation, or any nation so conceived, and so dedicated, can long endure. We are met on a great battle-field of that war. We have come to dedicate a portion of that field, as a final resting place for those who here gave their lives, that that nation might live. It is altogether fitting and proper that we should do this.

But, in a larger sense, we can not dedicate— we can not consecrate— we can not hallow— this ground. The brave men, living and dead, who struggled here, have consecrated it, far above our poor power to add or detract. The world will little note, nor long remember, what we say here, but it can never forget what they did here. It is for us the living, rather, to be dedicated here to the unfinished work which they who fought here, have, thus far, so nobly advanced. It is rather for us to be here dedicated to the great task remaining before us— that from these honored dead we take increased devotion to that cause for which they here gave the last full measure of devotion— that we here highly resolve that these dead shall not have died in vain— that this nation, under God, shall have a new birth of freedom— and that, government of the people, by the people, for the people, shall not perish from the earth.

Lincoln wrote out six copies of the Gettysburg Address, and five are known to survive, all with slight differences. The copy shown here is on display at the Old State Capitol in Springfield.

Lincoln," Douglass said later, "I was impressed with his entire freedom from popular prejudice against the colored race. He was the first great man that I talked with in the United States freely, who in no single instance reminded me of the difference between himself and myself, of the difference of color, and I thought that all the more remarkable because he came from a state where there were black laws."

After a quick lunch, Lincoln would read for a while, then turn to the piles of paperwork on his desk. One of his toughest jobs was reviewing court-martial sentences of Union soldiers—sleeping sentries, homesick runaways, cowards, deserters, and the like. He wanted to see that justice was done, yet he looked for excuses to pardon soldiers. He was reluctant to approve the death penalty,

Born a slave, Frederick Douglass escaped to freedom and became the most influential black leader of his time.

especially when a soldier had been sentenced to die before a firing squad for running away in the face of battle.

"Do you see those papers crowded in those pigeonholes [in my desk]?" Lincoln asked a visitor to his office. "They are the cases you call by that long title, 'cowardice in the face of the enemy.' I call them, for short, my 'leg cases.' I put it to you, and I leave it to you to decide for yourself: if Almighty God gives a man a cowardly pair of legs, how can he help their running away with him?"

Lincoln became famous for his last-minute pardons and reprieves. "The generals always wanted an execution carried out before it could possibly be brought before the president," a friend observed. "He was as tenderhearted as a girl."

Lincoln referred to himself as "pigeon-hearted." Even so, he tried to perform his duty as he saw it, and he did not always intervene. Large numbers of court-martialed soldiers actually were executed during the Civil War. But when he could think of a good reason to pardon, he pardoned, saying, "It rests me, after a hard day's work, that I can find some excuse for saving some poor fellow's life."

In late afternoon, Lincoln would go for a carriage ride with Mary, taking in the fresh air as they drove through the countryside, accompanied by a cavalry escort. Sometimes they stopped to chat with soldiers at an army mess or a military hospital before returning to the White House. If there was no official function that evening, the Lincolns might attend the opera or theatre, which Mary loved. Or Lincoln might relax with a small group of close friends, becoming his old self again, "the cheeriest of talkers, the riskiest of storytellers," as one friend said.

On most evenings, Lincoln returned to his office after dinner and worked late into the night by lamplight. His last chore before going to bed was to stop at the War Department telegraph room and read the latest dispatches from the front.

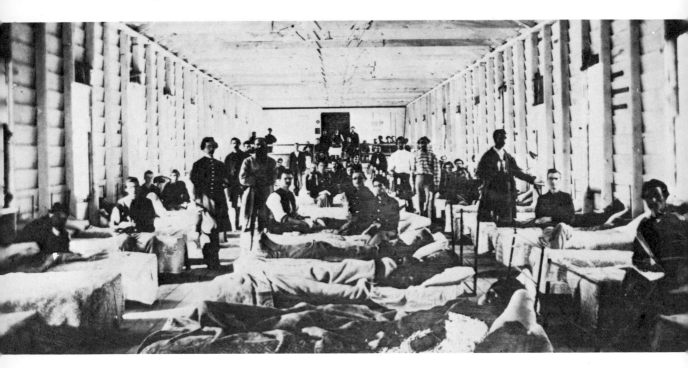

Wounded Union soldiers in a Washington hospital ward. Lincoln also visited Confederate wounded when he toured a hospital. According to Dr. Jerome Walker, ". . . He was just as kind, his handshakings just as hearty, his interest just as real for the welfare of the men, as when he was among our own soldiers."

On the Western front, Union armies had been winning a string of victories. On July 4, 1863—the day after the battle at Gettysburg—the fortified city of Vicksburg, the last important Confederate stronghold on the Mississippi, had surrendered to General Ulysses S. Grant. By the time of Lincoln's Gettysburg Address, Grant's armies were fighting their way through Tennessee, heading for Georgia and the heart of the Confederacy. Grant had emerged as the one commander the president could count on.

Early in 1864, Lincoln called the whiskered, cigar-smoking general to Washington and appointed him as the new general in chief of all Union armies.

Together, Grant and Lincoln worked out a plan to smash the Confederacy. They would launch coordinated offensives on all fronts, pounding at the rebels from every direction. In the East, Grant would personally direct a new drive against Lee's troops in Virginia, pushing toward the rebel capital at Richmond. In the West, Union forces under General William Tecumseh Sherman would advance from Tennessee into Georgia to strike at the crucial railway center of Atlanta. Then Sherman would drive north toward Virginia, squeezing the Confederacy in a pincer. Lincoln was hopeful. "Grant is the first general I have had," he said. "You

Ulysses S. ("Unconditional Surrender") Grant, Lincoln's favorite commander. He became general in chief in 1864.

know how it has been with all the rest. They wanted me to be the general. I am glad to find a man who can go ahead without me."

In May, 1864, the mightiest offensive of the war began. Grant marched into Virginia, but he met stubborn resistance from Lee's newly rebuilt army in a densely wooded area called the Wilderness. "I propose to fight it out on this line if it takes all summer," Grant declared. Unfortunately, that's what happened. After fighting three major battles near Richmond, Grant was unable to take the city. And his losses were staggering. About fifty-four thousand Union soldiers were killed or wounded during the Wilderness campaign. "Those poor fellows," Lincoln grieved, "this suffering, this loss of life."

Throughout the North, people were shocked by the death toll. Once again a cry went up to end the slaughter and bring the boys home. With all his other troubles, Lincoln now had to worry about the presidential election scheduled for 1864. Northern Democrats were determined to turn the president out of office. And there were some Republicans, members of Lincoln's own party, who talked of dumping him in favor of another candidate. They felt that Lincoln wasn't pushing the war vigorously enough, that he would be too easy on the South once the war was over, that in any case, he was too unpopular to win reelection.

Lincoln wanted to stay in office. Reelection alone would show that the people approved of his emancipation policy. He felt that he was "not entirely unworthy to be entrusted with the place" he had occupied since 1861. Most Republicans still supported the president, and now he exerted all his presidential powers of patronage and persuasion to rally the party and whip reluctant Republicans into line. In June, he was nominated for a second term by a National Union convention representing both Republicans and "war Democrats."

Confederate General Robert E. Lee.

Then the Democrats nominated their candidate—General George B. McClellan, the very same McClellan that Lincoln had dismissed as commander of the Union armies. McClellan ran against Lincoln on a peace platform, promising to stop the fighting right away and restore both the Union and slavery.

The summer of 1864 was the most dismal period of Lincoln's presidential career. People in the North were weary of the constant calls for more men, the growing casualty lists, the lack of progress. Friends and foes alike felt certain that Lincoln could not win the election. Some Republicans appealed to the president to step down in favor of a stronger candidate, and Lincoln himself

A political cartoon from the campaign of 1864 shows Lincoln, General McClellan, and Jefferson Davis fighting over the Union.

believed that he might lose. In a secret memorandum, he outlined his plans to hand over power in an orderly manner should the election go against him. "It seems exceedingly probable that this administration will not be reelected," he wrote.

As the election approached, there was good news—sensational news! Down in Georgia, General Sherman had finally pushed his way to Atlanta, and after a long siege, the city had surrendered. "Atlanta is ours," Sherman reported. The general ordered an evacuation of the city and had his troops destroy everything of military value—warehouses, factories, and army depots.

With Atlanta in flames, Sherman set out on a devastating march across Georgia, destroying fields and driving off livestock, bringing fire and ruin to everything in his path. Up in Virginia, cavalry troops under General Philip Sheridan were battering rebel

William Tecumseh Sherman led the Union advance into Georgia. An advocate of total war, Sherman declared: "We are not only fighting hostile armies, but a hostile people, and must make old and young, rich and poor, feel the hard hand of war."

forces in the Shenandoah Valley. Grant, meanwhile, was tightening his stranglehold on Richmond.

Union victories had come at last. By Election Day on November 8, it was clear that the end of the war was in sight. Lincoln's policies had been vindicated after all, and the president's Republican critics rallied around him. He won reelection by nearly half a million votes out of some four million cast.

Lincoln regarded the election as a mandate to push forward with his emancipation program. For months he had been urging Congress to pass a constitutional amendment that would outlaw slavery everywhere in America, not just in the rebel South, but in the loyal border states as well. Lincoln knew that his Emancipation Proclamation, a wartime measure, could be overturned at any time by the courts, by Congress itself, or by a future president. A constitutional amendment would get rid of slavery permanently.

As the winter of 1864 began, Lincoln put tremendous pressure on congressmen who opposed the amendment. The final vote came on January 31, 1865, when a cheering House of Representatives approved the Thirteenth Amendment, prohibiting slavery in the United States. Lincoln hailed the vote as a "great moral victory." William Lloyd Garrison, the Boston abolitionist who had often criticized Lincoln, now called him "presidential chainbreaker for millions of the oppressed."

A month later, on March 4, Lincoln stood before the Capitol and took his oath of office a second time. The pressures of the war showed clearly in the president's face. His features, a friend noted, were "haggard with care, tempest tossed and weatherbeaten."

Lincoln had thought long and deeply about the horrors of the war, trying to understand why the nation had been swept up into such violence, destruction, and death. At first the issue had seemed the salvation of the Union, but in the end, slavery had become the issue. The war had demonstrated that the Union could survive only if it were all free.

In his second Inaugural Address, Lincoln called slavery a hateful and evil practice—a sin in the sight of God. North and South alike shared the guilt of slavery, he declared. "This mighty scourge of war" was a terrible retribution, a punishment for allowing human bondage to flourish on the nation's soil. Now slavery was abolished, and the time had come for healing. Lincoln felt no malice, no hatred of the Southern people who had taken up arms against the United States:

"With malice toward none; with charity for all; with firmness in the right, as God gives us to see the right, let us strive on to finish the work we are in; to bind up the nation's wounds, to care for him who shall have borne the battle, and for his widow, and his orphan—to do all which may achieve and cherish a just and lasting peace among ourselves, and with all nations."

Even as Lincoln spoke, the Union war machine was sweeping toward a final victory. Sherman had marched from Atlanta to the sea, capturing the coastal city of Savannah, then slashing his way northward through the Southern heartland. Charleston, South Carolina, where the war had started, surrendered to Union forces in February. By March, Sherman had invaded North Carolina and was driving toward a rendezvous with Grant's armies in Virginia.

Richmond was still under siege. On April 2, Robert E. Lee notified Confederate President Jefferson Davis that he could no longer hold his lines. Richmond would have to be evacuated. That night, Davis and his government fled to Danville, Virginia, burning bridges and warehouses behind them. The flames swept through Richmond, setting hundreds of buildings ablaze. When Union troops marched into the city on April 3, their first job was to put out the fire.

The ruins of Charleston, South Carolina, at war's end.

The next day, Lincoln sailed up the James River with his son Tad and a small military escort, so he could see for himself the capital that had been the seat of rebellion for four years. A pall of smoke hung over the city as he stepped ashore, and fires were still burning. The only people in the streets were liberated slaves and black Union troops. They recognized Lincoln's tall, stovepipe-hatted form instantly.

Joyous black people flocked around the president, cheering and laughing, yelling his name, reaching for his hand. The growing crowd followed Lincoln and Tad as they stepped through the smouldering rubble and made their way to Jefferson Davis's head-quarters, the executive mansion of the Confederacy. Lincoln entered the abandoned building. He went to Davis's office. He stood before the desk that had belonged to the Confederate president. Then he sat down in Davis's chair, and the Union soldiers around him broke into cheers.

Fighting was still going on outside Richmond, but in a few days, it was all but over. On April 9, Generals Lee and Grant met face-to-face at a place called Appomattox Courthouse in Virginia. The two men exchanged pleasantries. Then Grant accepted Lee's sur-render. Lee's soldiers were to lay down their arms, but they could keep their horses so they could take them home for the spring planting. Grant sent a telegram to the president: "General Lee surrendered this morning on terms proposed by myself."

Jefferson Davis would refuse to admit defeat until his capture by Union troops in May. But for all practical purposes, the war was over.

The American Civil War had lasted almost exactly four years and cost the nation more than six-hundred thousand lives—about equal to the death toll in all other U.S. wars combined, before and since. Neither side had expected the war to last so long. And nei-ther side had expected it to end slavery.

1861.   *1862.*

1863.   *1864.*

The strain of war. A sampling of photographs taken during Lincoln's four years in office shows how the pressures and anxieties of the war became etched in his face.

April 10, 1865. A careworn president faces the camera for the last time in Alexander Gardner's Washington studio. As Gardner was taking the photograph, the glass-plate negative cracked across the top. After a single print was made, the negative broke completely.

SURRAT.   BOOTH.   HAROLD.

War Department, Washington, April 20, 1865,

 # $100,000 REWARD!

THE MURDERER

Of our late beloved President, Abraham Lincoln,

IS STILL AT LARGE.

$50,000 REWARD

Will be paid by this Department for his apprehension, in addition to any reward offered by Municipal Authorities or State Executives.

$25,000 REWARD

Will be paid for the apprehension of JOHN H. SURRATT, one of Booth's Accomplices.

$25,000 REWARD

Will be paid for the apprehension of David C. Harold, another of Booth's accomplices.

LIBERAL REWARDS will be paid for any information that shall conduce to the arrest of either of the above-named criminals, or their accomplices.

All persons harboring or secreting the said persons, or either of them, or aiding or assisting their concealment or escape, will be treated as accomplices in the murder of the President and the attempted assassination of the Secretary of State, and shall be subject to trial before a Military Commission and the punishment of DEATH.

Let the stain of innocent blood be removed from the land by the arrest and punishment of the murderers.

All good citizens are exhorted to aid public justice on this occasion. Every man should consider his own conscience charged with this solemn duty, and rest neither night nor day until it be accomplished.

EDWIN M. STANTON, Secretary of War.

DESCRIPTIONS.—BOOTH is Five Feet 7 or 8 inches high, slender build, high forehead, black hair, black eyes, and wears a heavy black moustache.

JOHN H. SURRAT is about 5 feet, 9 inches. Hair rather thin and dark; eyes rather light; no beard. Would weigh 145 or 150 pounds. Complexion rather pale and clear, with color in his cheeks. Wore light clothes of fine quality. Shoulders square; check bones rather prominent; chin narrow; ears projecting at the top; forehead rather low and square, but broad. Parts his hair on the right side; neck rather long. His lips are firmly set. A slim man.

DAVID C. HAROLD is five feet six inches high, hair dark, eyes dark, eyebrows rather heavy, full face, nose short, hand short and fleshy, feet small, instep high, round bodied, naturally quick and active, slightly closes his eyes when looking at a person.

NOTICE.—In addition to the above, State and other authorities have offered rewards amounting to almost one hundred thousand dollars, making an aggregate of about **TWO HUNDRED THOUSAND DOLLARS.**

Six days after this reward poster was issued, Lincoln's assassin was cornered in a Virginia barn and shot by pursuing army troops.

SEVEN

Who Is Dead in the White House?

"I know I'm in danger, but I'm not going to worry about it."

The president's friends were worried about his safety. They feared that rebel sympathizers would try to kidnap or kill him in a desperate attempt to save the Confederacy.

Lincoln had been living with rumors of abduction and assassination ever since he was first elected. Threatening letters arrived in the mail almost every day. He filed them away in a bulging envelope marked ASSASSINATION.

"I long ago made up my mind that if anyone wants to kill me, he will do it," he told a newspaper reporter. "If I wore a shirt of mail, and kept myself surrounded by a bodyguard, it would be all the same. There are a thousand ways of getting at a man if it is desired that he should be killed."

Even so, his advisors insisted on taking precautions. Soldiers camped on the White House lawn, cavalry troops escorted Lincoln on his afternoon carriage rides, and plainclothes detectives served as his personal bodyguards. He complained about the protection, but he accepted it. Thoughts of death were certainly on his mind. More than once, he had been troubled by haunting dreams.

He told some friends about a dream he had early in April, just before the fall of Richmond. In the dream, he was wandering through the halls of the White House. He could hear people sobbing, but as he went from room to room, he saw no one.

He kept on until he reached the East Room of the White House: "There I met with a sickening surprise. Before me was a . . . corpse wrapped in funeral vestments. Around it were stationed soldiers who were acting as guards; and there was a throng of people, some gazing mournfully upon the corpse, whose face was covered, others weeping pitifully. 'Who is dead in the White House?' I demanded of one of the soldiers. 'The President,' was his answer; 'he was killed by an assassin.' Then came a loud burst of grief from the crowd, which awoke me from my dream. I slept no more that night."

April 14, 1865, was Good Friday. Lee had surrendered just five days earlier, and Washington was in a festive mood. Lincoln arose early as usual, so he could work at his desk before breakfast. He was looking forward to the day's schedule. That afternoon he would tell his wife, "I never felt so happy in my life."

At eleven, he met with his cabinet. He had invited General Grant to attend the meeting as guest of honor. Most of the talk centered on the difficult problems of reconstruction in the conquered South. Lincoln emphasized again that he wanted no persecutions, "no bloody work." Enough blood had been shed.

"There are men in Congress," he said, "who possess feelings of hate and vindictiveness in which I do not sympathize and can not participate."

After lunch he returned to his office to review court-martial sentences. He revoked the death sentence of a Confederate spy. And he pardoned a deserter, signing his name with the comment, "Well, I think this boy can do us more good above ground than under ground."

Late in the afternoon he went for a carriage ride with Mary. That evening they would attend the theatre with another couple, but for the moment, they wanted some time to themselves. The war had been hard on both of them. Since Willie's death, Mary had been plagued by depression and imaginary fears, and at times, Lincoln had feared for his wife's sanity. As their carriage rolled through the countryside, they talked hopefully of the years ahead. "We must both be more cheerful in the future," Lincoln said. "Between the war and the loss of our darling Willie, we have been very miserable."

After dinner, Lincoln and Mary left for Ford's Theatre in the company of a young army major, Henry R. Rathbone, and his fiancee, Clara Harris. Arriving late, they were escorted up a winding stairway to the flag-draped presidential box overlooking the stage. The play had already started, but as Lincoln's party appeared in the box, the orchestra struck up "Hail to the Chief" and the audience rose for a standing ovation. Lincoln smiled and bowed. He took his place in a rocking chair provided for him by the management and put on a pair of gold-rimmed eyeglasses he had mended with a string. Mary sat beside him, with Major Rathbone and Miss Harris to their right.

The play was *Our American Cousin*, a popular comedy starring Laura Keene, who had already given a thousand performances in

Ford's Theatre, Washington, D.C.

the leading role. Lincoln settled back and relaxed. He laughed heartily, turning now and then to whisper to his wife. Halfway through the play, he felt a chill and got up to drape his black overcoat across his shoulders.

During the third act, Mary reached over to take Lincoln's hand. She pressed closer to him. Behind them, the door to the presidential box was closed but not locked. Lincoln's bodyguard that evening, John Parker, had slipped away from his post outside the door to go downstairs and watch the play.

The audience had just burst into laughter when the door swung open. A shadowy figure stepped into the box, stretched out his arm, aimed a small derringer pistol at the back of Lincoln's head, and pulled the trigger. Lincoln's arm jerked up. He slumped forward in his chair as Mary reached out to catch him. Then she screamed.

Actor John Wilkes Booth fires the fatal shot. Drawing from Harper's Weekly.

Major Rathbone looked up to see a man standing with a smoking pistol in one hand and a hunting knife in the other. Rathbone lunged at the gunman, who yelled something and slashed Rathbone's arm to the bone. Then the assailant leaped from the box to the stage, twelve feet below. One of his boot spurs caught on the regimental flag draped over the box. As he crashed onto the stage, he broke the shinbone of his left leg.

The assailant struggled to his feet, faced the audience, and shouted the motto of the commonwealth of Virginia: "*Sic semper tyrannis*"—(Thus always to tyrants). The stunned and disbelieving audience recognized him as John Wilkes Booth, the well-known actor. What was going on? Was this part of the play?

Booth hobbled offstage and out the stage door, where a horse was saddled and waiting. Twelve days later he would be cornered by federal troops and shot in a Virginia barn.

The theatre was in an uproar. People were shouting, standing on chairs, shoving for the exits, as Laura Keene cried out from the stage, "The president is shot! The president is shot!"

Two doctors rushed to the president's box. Lincoln had lost consciousness instantly. The bullet had entered his skull above his left ear, cut through his brain, and lodged behind his right eye. The doctors worked over him as Mary hovered beside them, sobbing hysterically. Finally, six soldiers carried the president out of the theatre and across the fog-shrouded street to a boardinghouse, where a man with a lighted candle stood beckoning. He was placed on a four-poster bed in a narrow room off the hallway. The bed wasn't long enough for Lincoln. He had to be laid diagonally across its cornhusk mattress.

Five doctors worked over the president that night. Now and then he groaned, but it was obvious that he would not regain consciousness. The room filled with members of the cabinet, with

Brandishing a knife, Booth leaps from the presidential box to the stage.
From Harper's Weekly.

At the stage door, Booth jumps onto a waiting horse and escapes. From Frank Leslie's Illustrated Newspaper.

congressmen and high government officials. Mary waited in the front parlor. "Bring Tad—he will speak to Tad—he loves him so," she cried. Tad had been attending another play that evening. Sobbing, "They killed my pa, they killed my pa," he was taken back to the White House to wait.

Robert Lincoln was summoned to join the hushed crowd around his father's bedside. Outside, cavalry patrols clattered down the street. Another assassin had just tried to murder Secretary of State William Seward. Everyone suspected that the attacks were part of a rebel conspiracy to murder several government officials and capture the city.

By dawn, a heavy rain was falling. Lincoln was still breathing faintly. Robert Lincoln surrendered to tears, then others in the room began to cry. At 7:22 A.M. on April 15, Lincoln died at the age of fifty-six. A doctor folded the president's hands across his chest. Gently he smoothed Lincoln's contracted face muscles, closed his eyelids, and drew a white sheet over his head. It was then that Secretary of War Edwin M. Stanton murmured, "Now he belongs to the ages."

The funeral was held in the East Room of the White House four days later, on April 19. Afterwards, the long funeral procession, led by a detachment of black troops, moved slowly up Pennsylvania Avenue to the muffled beat of drums and the tolling of church bells. When the procession reached the Capitol, Lincoln was carried inside to lie in state under the huge Capitol dome. The next day, thousands of people, black and white, soldiers and civilians, stood patiently in the rain, waiting to file past the open coffin.

On April 21, a funeral train set out on a sixteen-hundred mile journey to Illinois, carrying Abraham Lincoln home to his final resting place in Springfield. The train followed the same route Lincoln had taken when he came to Washington as president-elect. It stopped at major cities along the way, so mourners could again file past the coffin. Where it did not stop, men and women with their children stood silently along the route to watch the train pass.

On the night of May 2, the train left Chicago and puffed its way southward through the rain across the Illinois prairie. People had built bonfires along the railroad tracks, and they stood outlined against the glowing red flames at every prairie village and country crossroads as the funeral train passed through.

At 9 A.M. it approached Springfield with its bell tolling. It steamed slowly through the business center and pulled up at the station, where regiments of soldiers and delegations of officials

Lincoln's funeral procession on Pennsylvania Avenue, Washington, D.C., April 19, 1865.

were waiting to meet it. Tens of thousands of people jammed the streets around the station and stood on nearby rooftops. A military band began to play a funeral dirge. All the bells of Springfield tolled. Guns fired a salute. And the crowd fell silent as the train came to a stop.

Citizens of Springfield wait their turn to file into the state capitol to view Lincoln's body.

On the morning that Lincoln died, someone emptied the contents of his pockets and placed them in a box, which was wrapped in brown paper and tied with a string. Robert Lincoln passed the box on to his daughter, who presented it to the Library of Congress in 1937. Labeled "Do Not Open," it remained locked in a vault until 1976, when the string was untied and the paper unwrapped as the library staff looked on.

The morning he died, Lincoln had in his pockets a pair of small spectacles folded into a silver case; a small velvet eyeglass cleaner; a large linen handkerchief with *A. Lincoln* stitched in red; an ivory pocketknife trimmed with silver; and a brown leather wallet lined with purple silk. The wallet contained a Confederate five-dollar bill bearing the likeness of Jefferson Davis and eight newspaper clippings that Lincoln had cut out and saved. All the clippings praised him. As president, he had been denounced, ridiculed, and damned by a legion of critics. When he saw an article that complimented him, he often kept it.

One clipping found in Lincoln's wallet quotes the British reformer John Bright. Shortly before the presidential election of 1864, Bright wrote to the American newspaper publisher Horace Greeley and said:

"All those who believe that Slavery weakens America's power and tarnishes your good name throughout the world, and who regard the restoration of your Union as a thing to be desired . . . are heartily longing for the reelection of Mr. Lincoln. . . . they think they have observed in his career a grand simplicity of purpose and a patriotism which knows no change and does not falter."

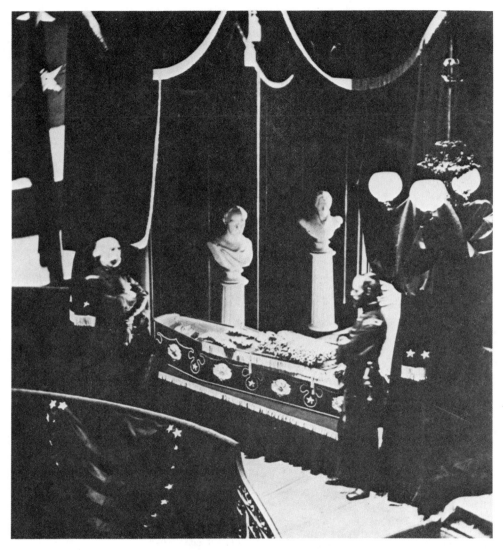

The president lies in state, flanked by honor guards. "I saw him in his coffin," wrote David R. Locke. "The face was the same as in life. Death had not changed the kindly countenance in any line. There was upon it the same sad look that it had worn always, though not as intensely sad as it had been in life. . . . It was the look of a worn man suddenly relieved."

"With malice toward none; with charity for all." Speaking from a temporary platform in front of the Capitol, Lincoln delivers his second Inaugural Address on March 4, 1865.

A Lincoln Sampler

Fellow citizens, I presume you all know who I am. I am humble Abraham Lincoln. I have been solicited by many friends to become a candidate for the legislature. My politics are short and sweet, like the old woman's dance. I am in favor of a national bank. I am in favor of the internal-improvements system and a high protective tariff. These are my sentiments and political principles. If elected, I shall be thankful; if not, it will be all the same.—*From an early political speech given at Pappsville, Illinois, July, 1832.*

"Every man is said to have his peculiar ambition. . . . I have no other so great as that of being truly esteemed of my fellow men, by rendering myself worthy of their esteem."—*From letter to the editor of* Sangamo Journal, *June 13, 1836.*

Let reverence for the laws be breathed by every American mother, to the lisping babe that prattles on her lap; let it be taught in schools, in seminaries, and in colleges; let it be written in Primmers [sic], spelling books, and in Almanacs; let it be preached from the pulpit, proclaimed in legislative halls, and enforced in halls of justice. And, in short, let it become the *political religion* of the nation.—*From speech to the Young Men's Lyceum of Springfield, January 27, 1838.*

The better part of one's life consists in his friendships.—*From letter to J. Gillespie, May 19, 1849.*

Resolve to be honest at all events; and if in your own judgment you cannot be an honest lawyer, resolve to be honest without being a lawyer.—*From notes for a law lecture, undated (1850s).*

No man is good enough to govern another man, *without that other's consent.* I say this is the leading principle—the sheet-anchor of American republicanism.—*From speech at Peoria, Illinois, October 16, 1854.*

Always bear in mind that your own resolution to succeed, is more important than any other one thing.—*From advice to an aspiring law student, Isham Reavis, November 5, 1855.*

I think the authors of [the Declaration of Independence] intended to include *all* men, but they did not intend to declare all men equal *in all respects.* They did not mean to say that all were equal in color, size, intellect, moral development, or social capacity. They defined with tolerable distinctness, in what respects they did consider all men created equal—equal in "certain inalienable rights, among which are life, liberty, and the pursuit of happiness." This they said, and this they meant.—*From speech at Springfield, June 26, 1857.*

If you once forfeit the confidence of your fellow citizens, you can never regain their respect and esteem. It is true that you may fool all of the people some of the time; you can even fool some of the people all of the time; but you can't fool all of the people all of the time.—*From speech at Clinton, Illinois, September 8, 1858.*

He who would *be* no slave, must consent to *have* no slave. Those who deny freedom to others, deserve it not for themselves; and, under a just God, cannot long retain it.—*From letter to H. L. Pierce and others, April 6, 1859.*

Writing, the art of communicating thoughts to the mind through the eye, is the great invention of the world. . . . enabling us to converse with the dead, the absent, and the unborn, at all distances of time and space.—*From lecture before the Springfield Library Association, February 22, 1860.*

Neither let us be slandered from our duty by false accusations against us, nor frightened from it by menaces of destruction to the Government nor of dungeons to ourselves. *Let us have faith that Right makes Might, and in that faith, let us, to the end, dare to do our duty as we understand it.—From address at Cooper Institute, New York, February 27, 1860.*

I am not ashamed to confess that twenty-five years ago I was a hired laborer, mauling rails, at work on a flatboat—just what might happen to any poor man's son. I want every man to have a chance—and I believe a black man is entitled to it—in which he can better his condition.—*From speech at New Haven, March 6, 1860.*

We [the North and the South] are not enemies, but friends. We must not be enemies. Though passion may have strained, it must not break, our bonds of affection. The mystic chords of memory, stretching from every battlefield and patriot grave to every living heart and hearthstone all over this broad land, will yet swell the chorus of the Union when again touched, as surely they will be, by the better angels of our nature.—*From First Inaugural Address, March 4, 1861.*

And, by virtue of the power and for the purpose aforesaid, I do order and declare that all persons held as slaves within said designated States and parts of States are, and henceforward shall be, free; and that the Executive Government of the United States, including the military and naval authorities thereof, will recognize and maintain the freedom of said persons.—*From Emancipation Proclamation, signed on January 1, 1863.*

Common-looking people are the best in the world; that is the reason the Lord makes so many of them.—*Remark by Lincoln, from diary of his secretary, John Hay, December 24, 1863.*

I claim not to have controlled events, but confess plainly that events have controlled me.—*From letter to A. G. Hodges, April 14, 1864.*

The people's will, constitutionally expressed, is the ultimate law for all.—*From response to a Serenade, October 19, 1864.*

Fondly do we hope—fervently do we pray—that this mighty scourge of war may speedily pass away.—*From Second Inaugural Address, March 4, 1865.*

I have always thought that all men should be free; but if any should be slaves, it should be first those who desire it for themselves, and secondly those who desire it for others. Whenever I hear anyone arguing for slavery, I feel a strong impulse to see it tried on him personally.—*From address to an Indiana Regiment, March 17, 1865.*

Bad promises are better broken than kept.—*From Lincoln's last public speech, April 11, 1865.*

—————————————————————————————————

The quotations that appear at the chapter openings are from the following sources: *Chapter 1,* letter to Jesse W. Fell, December 20, 1859. *Chapter 2,* interview with newspaperman John Locke Scripps, Lincoln's campaign biographer in 1860. *Chapter 3,* letter to Jesse W. Fell, December 20, 1859. *Chapter 4,* letter to A. G. Hodges, April 4, 1864. *Chapter 5,* Lincoln's comment at the official signing of the Emancipation Proclamation, January 1, 1863. *Chapter 6,* Lincoln's comment while traveling to Gettysburg, November 18, 1863. *Chapter 7,* Lincoln's remark to Secretary of State William Seward.

In Lincoln's Footsteps

Lincoln memorials, monuments, and museums attract millions of visitors every year. The historic sites listed here played an important part in Lincoln's life, career, and death. Hours and days are subject to change.

Abraham Lincoln Birthplace National Historic Site, 3 miles S of Hodgenville, KY, on U.S. 31E. (502) 358-3874. Located on the site Sinking Spring Farm, where Lincoln was born. An original Kentucky log cabin from the early nineteenth century has been reconstructed inside the Lincoln National Birthplace Memorial. Hours: 8 A.M.–6:45 P.M. June through August; 8 A.M.–4:45 P.M. rest of year. Closed: Christmas. For further information write: Superintendent, Route 1, Hodgenville, KY 42748.

Lincoln's Boyhood Home, 7 miles NE of Hodgenville, KY, on U.S. 31E. (502) 549–3741. Site of the Knob Creek farm where Abraham lived from age two to seven. A replica of the family log cabin contains historic items and antiques. Open daily, April 1 through November 1.

Lincoln Boyhood National Memorial and adjacent *Lincoln State Park,* 4 miles W of Santa Claus, IN, on State Route 162. (812) 937-4757. Site of the farm where Abraham did most of his growing up. Includes a reconstructed log cabin, a living pioneer farmstead with crops and animals of Lincoln's time, the graves of Lincoln's mother and sister, a school attended by Lincoln, and the Lincoln family church. Hours: 8 A.M.–5 P.M. Closed: Thanksgiving, Christmas, New Year's Day. For further information write: Superintendent, P.O. Box 1816, Lincoln City, IN 47522.

Lincoln's New Salem State Park, 20 miles NW of Springfield, IL, near Petersburg on State Route 97. (217) 632-7953. Reconstructed log-cabin village where Lincoln spent his early adult years. Features twenty-three timber buildings, including a sawmill and gristmill, the Rutledge tavern, the Lincoln–Berry store, the village school, and a stagecoach stop, along with oxen and farm animals, and craftspeople and guides in period clothing. Hours: 9 A.M.–5 P.M. summer; 8 A.M.–4 P.M. winter. Closed: Thanksgiving, Christmas, New Year's Day. For further information write: Superintendent, R.R. 1, Petersburg, IL 62675.

Lincoln Home National Historic Site, 8th and Jackson, Springfield, IL. (217) 492-4150. The only home that Lincoln ever owned. The family lived here for seventeen years, until their departure for Washington. Furnished with period pieces, including many associated with the Lincoln family. Hours: 8:30 A.M.–5 P.M. summer; hours may be reduced in winter. Closed: Thanksgiving, Christmas, New Year's Day.

Lincoln–Herndon Law Offices, 6th and Adams, Springfield, IL. (217) 782-4836. The only surviving building in which Lincoln maintained working law offices. Hours: 9 A.M.–5 P.M. Closed Thanksgiving, Christmas, New Year's Day.

Old State Capitol, 5th and Adams, Springfield, IL. (217) 782-4836. The center of Illinois government from 1839 to 1876. Restored and furnished as it was during Lincoln's legislative years. Hours: 9 A.M.–5 P.M. Closed: Thanksgiving, Christmas, New Year's Day.

Lincoln's Tomb State Historic Site, Oak Ridge Cemetery, Springfield, IL (217) 782-2717. Resting place of Lincoln and his family, built with public donations. Hours: 9 A.M.–5 P.M. Closed: Thanksgiving, Christmas, New Year's Day.

For more information about these and other Lincoln sites in Springfield, write: Springfield Visitors Bureau, 624 E. Adams, Springfield, IL 62701. Phone: (217) 789-2360. 1-800-545-7300. In IL: 1-800-356-7900.

For information about the Lincoln Heritage Trail, which includes historic sites in Kentucky, Indiana, and Illinois, write: Lincoln Heritage Trail Foundation, 702 Bloomington Road, Champaign, IL 61820.

Gettysburg National Military Park, Gettysburg, PA. (717) 334-1124. Site of the bloodiest battle in American history, and of Lincoln's most famous speech. Includes a National Cemetery and more than 1300 monuments, markers, and memorials. Visitors' Center Hours: 9 A.M.–5 P.M. Closed: Thanksgiving, Christmas, New Year's Day. Park roads are open from 6 A.M. to 10 P.M. year-round. For further information write: Superintendent, Gettysburg National Military Park, Gettysburg, PA 17325.

Ford's Theatre National Historic Site, 511 10th Street, N.W., Washington, D.C. (202) 426-6924. Restored to its original appearance on the night of April 14, 1865, when Lincoln, sitting in the presidential box, was shot by John Wilkes Booth. The Lincoln Museum in the basement contains many objects associated with Lincoln's life and career. Across the street, at number 516, is *Petersen House,* where Lincoln died on April 15. Hours: 9 A.M.–5 P.M. Closed: Christmas. During the theatrical season, Ford's Theatre is closed for afternoon matinees and rehearsals on Thursdays, Saturdays, and Sundays, but the Lincoln Museum and Petersen House remain open. For more information write: Site Manager, Ford's Theatre, 511 10th St., NW, Washington, D.C. 20004.

Books About Lincoln

More books have been written about Abraham Lincoln than any other American. The flood of books began with his death and now totals many thousands of titles covering every imaginable aspect of his life and career.

For the general reader, two standard biographies provide comprehensive accounts of Lincoln and his times: *With Malice Toward None: The Life of Abraham Lincoln* by Stephen B. Oates (New York, 1977) and *Abraham Lincoln: A Biography* by Benjamin P. Thomas (New York, 1952). A shorter biography, emphasizing Lincoln's early career, is *Abraham Lincoln and the Union* by Oscar and Lilian Handlin (New York, 1980).

Popular discussions of Lincoln myths, legends, and controversies include *Abraham Lincoln: The Man Behind the Myths* by

Stephen B. Oates (New York, 1984) and *The Lincoln Nobody Knows* by Richard N. Current (New York, 1958). An absorbing work for reference and browsing is *The Abraham Lincoln Encyclopedia* by Mark E. Neely Jr. (New York, 1981). Among the many illustrated books about Lincoln, some standouts are *Lincoln: A Picture Story of His Life* by Stefan Lorant (New York, 1969), *The Face of Lincoln*, compiled and edited by James Mellon (New York, 1979), and *Twenty Days* by Dorothy Meserve Kunhardt and Philip B. Kunhardt Jr. (New York, 1965), a vivid picture of the assassination and the mourning period that followed.

For an introduction to Lincoln's own writings, see *Abraham Lincoln: A Documentary Portrait Through His Speeches and Writings*, edited by Don E. Fehrenbacher (New York, 1964). The definitive edition of Lincoln's writings is *The Collected Works of Abraham Lincoln*, edited by Roy P. Basler, Marion Dolores Pratt, and Lloyd A. Dunlap (8 volumes plus index, New Brunswick, N.J. 1953–55; supplementary volume, 1974). The definitive work on Lincoln photographs is *Lincoln in Photographs: An Album of Every Known Pose*, by Charles Hamilton and Lloyd Ostendorf (Norman, Oklahoma, 1963).

Acknowledgments
and Picture Credits

For special help with the research for this book, I am indebted to Frank J. Dempsey, executive librarian, Arlington Heights Memorial Library, Arlington Heights, Illinois, my wise and witty guide to Lincoln country; Dr. George Weller of Owensboro, Kentucky, my fellow traveler to Lincoln's birthplace and boyhood homes; Thomas F. Schwartz, curator of the Lincoln Collection, Illinois State Historical Library, Springfield, who invited me to enter the Lincoln vault and feast my eyes on original documents; and Daniel R. Weinberg of the Abraham Lincoln Book Shop in Chicago, who helped me chart my initial course through the Lincoln literature.

Grateful thanks also to Grace L. Dinkins, Office of Rights and Reproductions, National Portrait Gallery; Judy Johnson, Lincoln Memorial University, Harrogate, Tennessee; Mark E. Neely, Jr., Louis A. Warren Lincoln Library and Museum, Fort Wayne, Indiana; Ann Shumard, Frederick Meserve Collection, National Portrait Gallery; Linda Ziemer, Chicago Historical Society; and the unfailingly helpful staffs of the Prints and Photographs Division, Library of Congress, and the Still Pictures Branch, National Archives.

The photographs and prints in this book are from the following sources and are used with their permission:

Abraham Lincoln Museum Collection, Lincoln Memorial University: page 10.

Chicago Historical Society: pages 18 (Photograph by Larry E. Hemenway), 34 (top), 63, 81 (bottom; Photograph by Brady).

Illinois State Historical Library: pages 8, 12, 17, 19 (both), 21, 29, 31 (both), 33, 34 (bottom), 38, 42, 44, 57, 58 (both), 62, 71, 78, 103, 104, 110, 118, 122, 125, 129, 131.

Library of Congress: pages ii, 3, 6, 13, 15, 23, 26 (both), 47, 49, 64 (left), 65 (left), 66, 75, 79, 87, 88, 97, 106, 114, 116 (top right), 116 (bottom left), 123, 126, 128.

Louis A. Warren Lincoln Library and Museum, Fort Wayne, Indiana: pages 40, 64 (right), 65 (right), 116 (top left).

Massachusetts Historical Society: page 95 (bottom).

National Archives: pages 51 (bottom), 54 (top), 69 (bottom), 73, 76, 81 (top), 83 (all photos), 92, 95 (top), 99, 100, 109, 111, 132.

National Portrait Gallery, Smithsonian Institution: pages x, 90, 107, 116 (bottom right), 117. Frederick Meserve Collection, National Portrait Gallery: pages ix, 69 (top).

The New-York Historical Society: page 51 (top).

New York Public Library: page 54 (bottom).

Index

Numbers in *italics* refer to pages with illustrations.